# Marshal Tito and Nicolae Ceaușescu: The Lives and Legacies of the Eastern Bloc's Most Notorious Non-Soviet Leaders

## By Charles River Editors

Ceaușescu and Tito

# About Charles River Editors

**Charles River Editors** is a boutique digital publishing company, specializing in bringing history back to life with educational and engaging books on a wide range of topics. Keep up to date with our new and free offerings with this 5 second sign up on our weekly mailing list, and visit Our Kindle Author Page to see other recently published Kindle titles.

We make these books for you and always want to know our readers' opinions, so we encourage you to leave reviews and look forward to publishing new and exciting titles each week.

# Introduction

"Tito did not like Ceaușescu personally, because when they went hunting wild boars together, Ceaușescu cheated and broke the rules. He once took a shot at a boar, and having missed it, fired at it a second time after the boar had moved out of Ceaușescu's and into Tito's field of fire. Tito then killed the boar with his first shot, but Ceaușescu falsely claimed that he too had hit the boar with his shot. 'In that case, your shot must have gone up the hole under the boar's tail,' said Tito sarcastically. When they went hunting together again a few year later, Ceaușescu again claimed to have killed a boar when it was in fact Tito who had shot it." = Jasper Ridley, *Tito: A Biography*

"No country of people's democracy has so many nationalities as this country has. Only in Czechoslovakia do there exist two kindred nationalities, while in some of the other countries there are only minorities. Consequently in these countries of people's democracy there has been no need to settle such serious problems as we have had to settle here. With them the road to socialism is less complicated than is the case here. With them the basic factor is the class issue, with us it is both the nationalities and the class issue. The reason why we were able to settle the nationalities question so thoroughly is to be found in the fact that it had begun to be settled in a revolutionary way in the course of the Liberation War, in which all the nationalities in the country participated, in which every national group made its contribution to the general effort of liberation from the occupier according to its capabilities. Neither the Macedonians nor any other national group which until then had been oppressed obtained their national liberation by decree.

They fought for their national liberation with rifle in hand. The role of the Communist Party lay in the first place in the fact that it led that struggle, which was a guarantee that after the war the national question would be settled decisively in the way the communists had conceived long before the war and during the war. The role of the Communist Party in this respect today, in the phase of building socialism, lies in making the positive national factors a stimulus to, not a brake on, the development of socialism in our country. The role of the Communist Party today lies in the necessity for keeping a sharp lookout to see that national chauvinism does not appear and develop among any of the nationalities. The Communist Party must always endeavour, and does endeavour, to ensure that all the negative phenomena of nationalism disappear and that people are educated in the spirit of internationalism." – Tito

"Esteemed chairman of the court, today we have to pass a verdict on the defendants Nicolae Ceaușescu and Elena Ceaușescu who have committed the following offenses: Crimes against the people. They carried out acts that are incompatible with human dignity and social thinking; they acted in a despotic and criminal way; they destroyed the people whose leaders they claimed to be. Because of the crimes they committed against the people, I plead, on behalf of the victims of these two tyrants, for the death sentence for the two defendants." – An excerpt of chief prosecutor Dan Voinea's statements during Ceaușescu's trial

The World War II era produced many leaders of titanic determination, men whose strengths and weaknesses left an extraordinary imprint on historical affairs. The struggle between massively divergent ideologies, exacerbated by huge social changes affected by the world's technological metamorphosis into the machine age, catapulted some individuals unexpectedly onto the world stage.

Josip Broz Tito, better known to history as Marshal Tito, was undoubtedly one of these figures. Originally a machinist, Tito leveraged his success in the Communist Party of Yugoslavia (CPY) and a number of extraordinary strokes of luck into dictatorial rule over Yugoslavia for a span of 35 years. World War II proved the watershed that enabled him to secure control of the country, leading an ever more powerful army of communist partisans against both the Germans and other Yugoslav factions. During the war, SS leader Heinrich Himmler himself begrudgingly stated, "He has really earned his title of Marshal. When we catch him we shall kill him at once... but I wish we had a dozen Titos in Germany, men who were leaders and had such resolution and good nerves, that, even though they were forever encircled, they would never give in."

During his reign, Tito managed to quash the intense national feelings of the diverse groups making up the Yugoslavian population, and he did so through several methods. He managed to successfully play the two superpower rivals, the United States and Soviet Union, off against each other during the Cold War, and in doing so, he maintained a considerable amount of independence from both, even as he additionally received foreign aid to keep his regime afloat. All the while he remained defiant, once penning a legendary letter to Joseph Stalin warning the

Soviet dictator, "To Joseph Stalin: Stop sending people to kill me! We've already captured five of them, one of them with a bomb and another with a rifle... If you don't stop sending killers, I'll send a very fast working one to Moscow and I certainly won't have to send another."

Never afraid to use political murder when expedient, yet simultaneously outgoing and good-humored to those around him, Tito created a unique and unusual state between the Western democracies and the Eastern Bloc. Only with his death did the fabric of his "national communist" state tear asunder and age-old identities reassert themselves, bringing about a period of intense conflicts that produced a new equilibrium with ethnically-based successor states that cracked up the state he once led.

Nicolae Ceaușescu, one of the 20th century's most notorious dictators, was both typical and unusual. Outwardly he resembled a standard leader of a communist country in Eastern Europe during the Cold War, yet he was even more repressive and opulent than his contemporaries. In Romania itself, Ceaușescu led a life as an isolated outsider, notably less urbane than the Bucharest elite, and given that he was born in rural poverty to peasant parents, his rise was perhaps the unlikeliest of any of the communists of that generation.

As it turned out, circumstances presented themselves in a manner that led to his elevation, including the acquaintances he made whilst serving time in prison in the 1930s and 1940s, the rise of communism after World War II, and the Soviet occupation of a country that had previously banned the ideology. Ceaușescu was a compromise candidate when Romanian leader Gheorghe Gheorghiu-Dej died in 1965, and he initially appeared to be a liberal-minded, nationalist-orientated reformer. Ceaușescu did fit very easily into one stereotype, however, by proving that absolute power corrupts absolutely. From the early 1970s, he and his wife Elena constructed the most grotesquely personalized cult of dictatorship in the region, and while operating at the pinnacle of a highly corrupt pyramid, the couple bled their country dry with a succession of incompetent and warped policies. Ceaușescu's own father would say of him, "He tells nothing but lies." His son wasn't much more charitable, saying, "The new kind of politicians lie all the time. But my father was one of the old kind, more of a fanatic. He was driven by some kind of fanaticism. This belief that you can do good. It's a sort of madness."

By the end of the 1980s, communism was collapsing across Central Europe and Eastern Europe, but whereas the popular unrest that toppled the authoritarian regimes in other countries triggered a peaceful transition of power, in Romania, the anger and frustration was so acute that the Ceaușescu's were captured, tried, and executed within the space of a few tumultuous days in December 1989. True to form, he made wild statements in his defense, insisting during the trials, "It is a lie that I made the people starve. A lie, a lie in my face. This shows how little patriotism there is, how many treasonable offenses were committed.... At no point was there such an upswing, so much construction, so much consolidation in the Romanian provinces. I guaranteed that every village has its schools, hospitals and doctors. I have done everything to create a decent and rich life for the people in the country, like in no other country in the world." Ultimately, by the end of his life, Ceaușescu had already left his mark as one of the 20th century's most infamous despots.

*Marshal Tito and Nicolae Ceaușescu: The Lives and Legacies of the Eastern Bloc's Most Notorious Non-Soviet Leaders* examines the careers of the two leaders, and how they compared and contrasted with each other. Along with pictures of important people and places, you will learn about Tito and Ceaușescu like never before.

Marshal Tito and Nicolae Ceaușescu: The Lives and Legacies of the Eastern Bloc's Most Notorious Non-Soviet Leaders

## Tito's Early Life

"In the most trying hours, through dismal nights and endless interrogations and maltreatment, during days of killing solitude in cells and close confinement, we were always sustained by the hope that all these agonies were not in vain, that there was a strong and mighty country, however far away, in which all the dreams for which we were fighting had been fulfilled. For us it was the homeland of the workers, in which labour was honoured, in which love, comradeship, and sincerity prevailed." - Tito

Originating in Kumrovec, a Croatian village in the shadow of Cesargrad Castle, Josip Broz Tito lived in one of the small town's best houses, that of his parents Franjo Broz and Marija Javeršek. Though his forefathers had built up a relatively large holding of 15 acres and bequeathed him a horse and cart, Franjo Broz found himself in an untenable situation as cheap foreign grain pushed down farm income. He took to drink, and progressive alcoholism only made the family's success melt away faster. Tito himself, in his later surprisingly frank and humorous autobiography, described his parents and the decline of the Broz fortunes: "My father was a wiry man with black curly hair and an aquiline nose. […] Going to  the villages across the Sutla, Franjo became acquainted with a sixteen-year-old Slovene girl called Marija […] She was a tall, blonde woman, with an attractive face. […] A hard life awaited my parents. […] When the debts became intolerable, the soft and good-natured Franjo gave it up and took to drinking, and the whole family burden fell upon my mother, an energetic woman." (Dedijer, 1953, 12-13).

**Janez Novak's picture of Tito's birthplace**

Born on May 7th, 1892, the future Marshal Tito attended school sporadically. Though he enjoyed education and received commendations from his teachers when he attended his classes, Josip faced opposition from his parents, who believed schooling was useless compared to farm work. Reversing truancy's usual pattern, Tito went "truant" from home to attend school.

Outside of school, Tito proved adventurous, restlessly energetic, and combative. He learned how to be an adept rider at an early age and showed immense fondness for dogs, particularly his favorite pet, a sheepdog named Polak. This animal guarded the younger Broz children reliably and lived to the age of 16.

He also led the local boys in raids on orchards and similar activities, usually playing the part of leader due to his daring and extreme energy. He participated in playful skirmishes simulating the 1573 attack on Cesargrad Castle by Matija Gubec's rebels, with the boys decorating their hats with rooster feathers in the same manner as the bellicose Croatian peasants of some 300 years before. The castle still had a sinister reputation, since although the peasants seized it and killed the bailiff, Baroness Barbara Erdody escaped to return later with fresh troops and slaughter hundreds of the rebels. Tito recalled, "Three centuries later […] whenever as children we awoke at night, our mother threatened that the Black Queen of Cesargrad would take us away if we did not go back to sleep at once." (West, 2012, 26).

History repeated itself in 1903 with a brief, minor rebellion against the Austro-Hungarians. Then 11 years old, Tito watched the local people tearing down Hungarian flags in protest over a new tax. Soldiers soon arrived to restore Austro-Hungarian rule, and a quartet of Hungarian soldiers received a billet in Franjo Broz's house for four weeks.

As Tito reached his early teens, Franjo Broz wanted to send him overseas to the United States in search of fame and fortune, but poverty prevented him. When he reached the age of 15, Tito went to the town of Sisak, where his soldier cousin Jurica Broz found a job for him as a waiter at a cafe. Tito only stayed at the cafe long enough to save some money, whereupon he set out to find work more suited to his tastes.

Fascinated by railroads and locomotives, Tito tried to find work on a train but failed, so in order to satisfy his craving for mechanical work in some fashion, he enrolled for a three-year apprenticeship with Master Nikolas Karas, a local locksmith of Czech extraction. The job suited Tito, though he sometimes neglected it in his newly discovered passion of reading adventure novels – including Sherlock Holmes stories by Sir Arthur Conan Doyle – and history books: "Josip enjoyed his three years as an apprentice. The work was hard, but he liked it. He liked the smell of oil, the whir of the lathes and drills and the sparks which flew from the molten metal. He liked, above all, the feeling that he was making something." (MacLean, 1957, 9).

The huge Karas found Tito, late in his apprenticeship, neglecting a running drill (which broke) in order to read a Sherlock story. The Czech punched his Croatian apprentice in the face, prompting Tito to run away and join the workers at a brickyard. The police found him almost immediately and threw him in prison for breaking his apprenticeship agreement, but Karas sent him a large meal, then appeared in person to secure Tito's release, after which he finished his apprenticeship without incident.

Tito read his first socialist newspaper, *Slobodna Reč*, in 1909, and when he finished his apprenticeship in 1910 he moved to Zagreb (then named Agram), where he joined the Metal Workers' Union. The young Croatian showed great dedication to the union, attending meetings or demonstrations, and paying his back dues promptly whenever he found work after a period of involuntary unemployment.

Initially, Tito's personal ambition did not extend beyond buying himself fashionable clothing, a fixation undoubtedly due to his frequent raggedness as a child. He saved up a considerable sum from his first independent work to purchase the fanciest suit available for a triumphant return home at Christmas. However, shortly before the holiday trip, he returned from work to find the door of his tiny apartment forced open and his expensive tailored suit stolen, never to be retrieved.

Low-cost American grain exports badly damaged the Croatian economy at the time, forcing Tito to travel from place to place in search of work. His skill and Union membership ensured that he never remained without a paying job for an excessive length of time. He eventually found relatively stable work at a metalworking factory in Kamnik. At this time, Tito also joined a patriotic gymnastic club, "Soko" or "Falcon," though less because of its anti-Habsburg tendencies than from his own personal sartorial eccentricity: "I liked their colored uniforms and feather-tipped caps. I bought one on installments and took part in every parade, marching at a smart gait behind the band." (West, 2012, 32).

Tito learned to speak Czech and German fluently during these early years, and he showed a taste for women which became one of his defining traits for much of the rest of his life.

In 1913, he secured a much better job as a skilled mechanic at the Daimler factory near Vienna, and the Daimler Works soon employed him as a test driver: "The work here interested me more than in any other factory. I even became a test driver, running the big, powerful cars with their heavy brasswork, rubber-bulb horns and outside hand-brakes, to put them through their paces. These were useful experiences." (Dedijer, 1953, 30).

As a subject of the Austro-Hungarian Empire, Tito received his mustering orders later in 1913 at age 21, ending his happy sojourn at Daimler. He asked to be assigned to the 25th Domobran Regiment so that he could receive his orders in Croatian rather than Hungarian. He received specialized training in military skiing, useful in the mountainous Balkans, and, thanks to his continued energy and confidence, he eventually received non-commissioned officer training and the rank of Sergeant Major (Stabsfeldwebel).

In his later reminiscences, Tito claimed that the Austrian army concerned itself mainly with unimportant details, such as learning the names of the royal family or performing intricate drill maneuvers that looked splendid on the parade ground but offered little advantage on the battlefield. While some of this undoubtedly came in hindsight from the perspective of a communist attempting to blacken the reputation of the loathed nobility, Austrian forces in World War I fought with considerably less skill than German soldiers. The Germans showed themselves tough, resourceful men with considerable fighting prowess and high morale, while the Austrian troops panicked more frequently and often fought indifferently.

One curious punishment meted out to soldiers, described by Tito, consisted of capturing a frog and placing it inside a chalk circle on the floor. The soldier was then obliged to keep the frog inside the circle under threat of heavier penalties, for however long his commander decided. Other soldiers might be forced to stand in front of their comrades for hours, loudly repeating "I am stupid, I am stupid."

Tito's NCO rank eventually insulated him from these petty, time-consuming tyrannies, enabling him to study military science, learn skiing on Mount Sljeme, and practicing the role of squad leader. He also learned fencing, deemed appropriate for a "gentleman" – even a sergeant – and claimed to have won first place in competitive regimental fencing matches.

## World War I and Revolution

"Wars of conquest are negative, the subjugation and oppression of other nations is negative, economic exploitation is negative, colonial enslavement is negative, and so on. All these things are accounted negative by Marxism and condemned. All these phenomena of the past can, it is true, be explained, but from our point of view they can never be justified." - Tito

Tito's obligatory military service occurred precisely in time to land him in the thick of World War I. On June 28th, 1914, a Serbian, Gavrilo Princip, shot and killed the heir to the Austrian throne, Archduke Franz Ferdinand, and his wife Sophie, launching the conflict. The Austrian forces entered Serbia, only to be handed several stinging, large-scale defeats by the Serbs. In some of these encounters, largely ignored by later history, the Serbs completely routed whole Austrian armies.

Gallant and fierce as the Serbs showed themselves, numbers eventually told against them, but by that time Russian troops entered the eastern front war in hordes. Tito's regiment found itself deployed to plug a gap left when the Russians fought their way over the Carpathian Mountains to menace Budapest. With the weather already frigid, the Croatian soldiers suffered immensely, dying of cold in considerable numbers. The clothing issued soon fell apart, while the low-quality greatcoats kept out no moisture despite alleged waterproofing.

Nonetheless, Josip noted that the Russians suffered even worse hardships due to equipment inferior even to that of the Austrians. He observed some Russian units with bayonets but no rifles to fix them to. These men charged, unsupported by artillery, in an effort to close to melee range, only to be mowed down by Croatian rifle fire.

During the war, Tito developed something of a knack for leading scouting expeditions and small raids as the lines became relatively fixed over the winter. His platoon slipped past the Russian front lines repeatedly to gather intelligence and spread chaos in the enemy rear. In the course of one expedition, the men surprised 80 Russian soldiers sleeping in a house with no sentries on guard and managed to capture the entire group, shepherding them back to Austrian lines before sunup.

With food rations scarce despite Tito's efforts, the occasional "windfall" of meat became a memorable occasion. Tito later recounted the unusual culinary technique used by one of his men after acquiring a chicken: "My orderly, a Tsigane [...] took the hen and killed it and, after cleaning out the entrails, wrapped it up, feathers and all, in a coat of clay. Then he covered it up in hot ashes. When the clay had been baked as hard as earthenware, he withdrew it from the ashes and struck it with his rifle butt. The clay dropped off with the feathers stuck to it, and what presented itself to our eyes was chicken baked to a tender, tempting brown." (Dedijer, 1953, 34).

As warmer spring weather began to return to the Balkans in the early months of 1915, the Russians renewed their Carpathian offensive, including in the sector held by Tito's regiment. Easter fell on March 22nd, and the regimental officers all left the front lines to celebrate the holiday in whatever style they could manage, but the Russians continued fighting. A Russian attack pushed back an Austrian unit on the Croatians' flank, opening a considerable gap between the two formations. While a Russian infantry unit engaged the Croatian troops in front to keep them occupied a strong force of Circassian cavalry pounced on the undefended gap.

The Circassian lancers in their tall sheepskin hats charged the rear of the Croatians. A slaughter ensued, during which some of the Croatians continued fighting. Others threw down their weapons to surrender, but the Circassians gleefully butchered these men alongside their more pugnacious comrades. Two Circassians attacked Tito, who attempted to fend off one man using his rifle and bayonet. A second lancer rushed him from behind, plunging his spear into Tito's body and narrowly missing his heart. The killing continued until the Russian infantry moved forward and took the remaining men prisoner. The men picked up Tito's unconscious body and carried him with them into captivity. This ended his direct participation in World War I's combat.

Though it proved not to be fatal, Tito's wound took an extended period to heal with essentially pre-modern medical care. The Russians sent him to a hospital in Sviyazhsk, a town in Tatarstan on the banks of the Volga River. Tito remained in the hospital for 13 months, first suffering from his wound, then a crippling case of pneumonia, and finally with typhus caught from infected louse bites. At one point in his delirium, Tito began cursing and swearing at an icon on the wall above him in the fevered belief the painted man was a thief about to steal his clothes. The other prisoners later described these ravings to him. At one point, a nurse tied a red ribbon to his bed to indicate a dying man, but Tito pulled through.

**A picture of the Uspensko-Bogorodichny monastery, the site where Broz recovered during the war**

Once he recovered enough to shake off his hallucinations, Tito set about learning Russian with the help of books brought to him by two local girls, and by the middle of 1916, Tito had finally recovered enough to start working again. He moved to Ardatov, where a motorized mill existed, and his mechanical skills soon earned him a post maintaining the mill equipment. The mill owner, wanting to retain Tito's services, tried to persuade him to marry one of his daughters, but the Croatian politely refused.

Soon after that, however, the Russians moved Tito again, this time to the Kungur prisoner of war camp near Perm. The prisoners there worked at repairing the Trans-Siberian Railway, and Tito, as an NCO, commanded the other men, all private soldiers. Though the men received payment for their work, the amount proved insufficient to buy warm clothing or sufficient food, so some of the prisoners died on an almost daily basis. Eventually, Red Cross aid packages started arriving, containing much-needed food and clothing. The lot of the prisoners improved briefly as first American Red Cross and then Swedish Red Cross aid reached them. Then the packages tapered off again. Investigating, Tito found out that the Russian section boss sold the parcels after stealing them. He complained to the local Red Cross representative, which stopped the theft but won the hatred of the section boss, whom Tito called "a sinister figure."

The Russian obtained his revenge in early 1917 when several workers stayed in their barracks late to repair their boots. He claimed this indicated Tito falsified everything. A group of Cossacks dragged the Croatian away to the town prison, threw him into the cellar, and beat him savagely with their knouts.

After Tito remained in the prison for several days, however, the February 1917 overthrow of Czar Nicholas II occurred and the Russian Revolution began. The Kungur townspeople stormed the prison to free all prisoners, which allowed Tito to leave and return to the POW camp. A Polish Bolshevik, also freed from prison, had become his friend during their shared time in the jail. The section overseer managed to have Tito returned to the prison after a while, this time for an extended period, but his Polish friend managed to contrive his escape with the help of several other Bolsheviks and arranged for him to flee to St. Petersburg, or Leningrad, where he could hide at the residence of the Pole's son.

Tito continued his adventures through the slowly disintegrating chaos of Imperial Russia's final days. He reached St. Petersburg in summer 1917 during the July Days, when tension between workers and the provisional government reached a flashpoint. 500,000 workers began a series of peaceful demonstrations under Bolshevik leadership, and soldiers dispersed the marches with heavy machine gun fire, mowing down some 700 individuals. A series of arrests followed, temporarily breaking Bolshevik power in the city.

Tito later claimed that he participated in the demonstrations and fled from machine gun fire along with other men. Regardless, police came for the Pole's son, but Tito managed to escape, sleeping under St. Petersburg's bridges for a few days before setting out for the Finnish border. He planned to emigrate to the United States if he could reach Finland, but the border guards caught him and returned him to St. Petersburg. In a radio talk in 1976, Tito revealed his original plan to go to America and added, "Had I done it, I would have become a millionaire." (West, 2012, 44).

Due to his fluent Russian and Slavic appearance, Tito experienced some difficulty persuading the authorities of his identity as an "Austrian" POW and not an escaping Russian revolutionary. The police temporarily imprisoned him in the Peter and Paul Fortress, and even when they finally believed his story, his situation scarcely improved: "The River Neva rose to the very windowpanes. The cell was all stone, and running with rats. Three weeks later I was banished back to Kungur, to the Urals. I was extremely reluctant to return to this place, knowing well that nothing good awaited me there, and I watched for an opportunity to escape from the train." (Dedijer, 1953, 38).

**Dmitry Mottl's picture of the Peter and Paul Fortress**

**Andrew Shiva's aerial photo of the fortress**

Tito slipped away from his guards at Ekaterinburg with the simple ruse of asking the man on duty to fetch him water for tea, then merging into the crowd. He traveled on a passenger train, using his fluent, unaccented Russian to inform soldiers who boarded at various stops in search of him that he had seen no Austrian fugitives. Ultimately, Tito rode the train all the way into Siberia, arriving at Atamansky Hutor just as the October Revolution occurred. He identified himself as an Austrian POW with Bolshevik and working class sympathies to the Soviet workers who swarmed onto the train with rifles and pistols. Along with many other foreigners, Tito joined the Red Guard, partly as way to reduce the chances of being shot as a counterrevolutionary spy.

The Soviets provided the Red Guards with weapons, clothing, and food, but they still did not completely trust them. Requests to be sent to the front by the Red Guards met with friendly refusal by the Soviet Russians, who doubtless assumed the men would immediately desert back to the Austro-Hungarian army. Thus, Tito found himself with a detail guarding the Marianovka railway station, deep in east Russia.

In 1918, the situation in Siberia abruptly changed, and it brought important changes in Tito's life as well. In 1917, he met a local girl, the 14 year old Pelageya Belousova, and the two formed a romantic attachment. The following year, one of the Provisional Government's military units, the Czech Corps, began moving towards the west to return to their home country, but an intercepted telegram from Trotsky seemed to indicate their safe conduct through Bolshevik territory might be a sham: "[E]very Czech who is found carrying a weapon anywhere along the route of the railway is to be shot on the spot." (Lincoln, 1999, 94). The Czechs accordingly attacked the nearest Bolsheviks, who happened to be the Red Guards at Marianovka railway station near Omsk, where Tito served. Tito managed to escape the slaughter with the aid of his girlfriend Pelageya Belousova and her family, first hiding with them and then with the nomadic Kirghiz living in the steppes south of Omsk. Tito's luck did not desert him, as the local chieftain, an owner of 2,500 horses named Hadji Isaj Djaksembayev, also owned one of the new mechanical mills with which the Croatian machinist enjoyed great familiarity.

**The Versailles State**

"I knew that many things were wrong... I witnessed a great many injustices... But it was my revolutionary duty at the time not to criticize and not to help alien propaganda against [the Soviet Union], for at that time it was the only country where a revolution had been carried out and where Socialism had been built. I considered that propaganda should not be made against that country; that my duty was to make propaganda in my own country for Socialism." - Tito

While the Czechs helped form the Siberian Government and then supported Admiral Alexander Kolchak's short-lived White Russian regime in Omsk, Tito joined fully in the Kirghiz lifestyle. His horsemanship skills enabled him to keep up with his swift-moving hosts, and he enjoyed wolf hunting with them, chasing down the carnivores and spearing them from horseback in defense of the extensive Kirghiz herds. At one point Tito tried raising a pair of wolf cubs, but they decamped to the wilderness as soon as they approached maturity.

**Kolchak**

The Red and White Russians fought viciously over the Omsk region throughout most of 1919. Finally, the Bolsheviks prevailed, ending Kolchak's reign and eventually his life. With the region back in the hands of the communists, Tito returned to Omsk, suffering robbery by a band of brigands on the way. In Omsk, he found Pelageya, now 16 years old, and married her.

With the Bolsheviks in charge of most of the country, the couple found themselves able to travel by rail to St. Petersburg, now renamed Petrograd. Quarantined in Narva, they eventually boarded the vessel *Lili Feuermann* to sail across the fogbound Baltic Sea to Stettin. Returning to Croatia by train, Tito and Pelageya, the latter now in the late stages of pregnancy, were arrested at the border as communists, but the police soon released them. They finally reached Tito's hometown of Kumrovic in early October 1920.

Tito's homecoming proved depressing. His mother, he discovered, had died in 1918, two years before his return. Meanwhile, his father no longer lived in the family house and now dwelt in

Jastrebarsko on the outskirts of Zagreb. Pelageya soon gave birth to a baby boy, but the child died after two days. Tito, his triumphant homecoming shattered, moved to Zagreb with his wife and found a job at a machine shop.

The Treaty of Versailles, imposing terms on the defeated Germans after World War I, established a large number of new countries out of the old empires. Most of these nations contained a strong ethnic majority, making them potentially stable long-term despite the scornful dismissal of older statesmen who labeled them "Versailles states." However, the Kingdom of the Serbs, Croats, and Slovenes represented something of a multicultural experiment from the first. In the early 1920s, the Serbs supported the creation of a unified Yugoslavia and the Croatians opposed it. The communists also disliked the idea of Yugoslavia, though this would change abruptly within a generation. A Carinthian newspaper seethed, "[T]he leaders of the American Slovenes and the Serbians agree in their demands for a single Yugoslav state. In addition to the agitation in representative bodies there is an insidious propaganda from man to man, woman to woman and even from child to child. At church and at school, the creed of the Yugoslav state is taught and the credulous population swears by its principles." (West, 1994, 48).

Communism took root rapidly in the Kingdom of the Serbs, Croats, and Slovenes. Winning 34% of the vote in Belgrade and 39% in Zagreb, the communists soon found themselves under temporary ban as far as activism went until the government created a new constitution, and in reprisal, a Bosnian communist killed the Minister of the Interior on July 21st, 1921, triggering an even more vigorous crackdown on communism. For his part, Tito delivered a fiery communist speech at the Zagreb Trade Unions meeting in November 1920. His machine shop employer immediately fired him, compelling Tito to move to a small town, Veliko Trojstvo, where his mechanical skills at fixing, maintaining, and operating the local mill outweighed his dangerous political convictions, keeping him employed through 1925.

Pelageya bore child after child, but all of them died from various ailments until the couple's last child together, a boy named Zarko. Tito soon felt confident enough to return to his open communist affiliation, achieving leadership of the Križevci District Committee of the Communist Party in 1924 while continuing to work at the mill.

**Tito and his family**

After delivering a belligerently communist speech and waving a red flag at a fellow union member's funeral, Tito found himself under arrest, and the police held him for eight days before releasing him. Moreover, the mill owner died in summer of 1925, and his nephew, the new owner, loathed communists. With the police watching him and ransacking his small apartment periodically for communist literature, Tito quit and moved again.

Tito's last job involving physical labor involved repairing torpedo boats in the port town of Kraljevica. He organized a cell of the Communist Party in the town and organized strikes so vigorously that he came to the attention of the Metalworkers' Union and various powerful communist organizations in Zagreb. He returned to the city in early 1927, became the leader of the communist Croatian Regional Committee, and henceforth devoted himself entirely to politics.

The background against which Tito worked witnessed monumental political changes. With the tensions between Serbs, Croatians, Slovenes, and other people who wished to live independently from the others making representative government progressively more difficult in postwar Yugoslavia, King Alexander stepped in, abolishing the Vidovan Constitution in 1929. From then on, he ruled as a "benevolent despot," using royal fiat to impose an uneasy unity on the country. Writing in 1949, the UCLA political science professor and historian Dr. Malbone Graham believed that this approach had worked, abolishing the ethnic and nationalist feelings of the various groups inside Yugoslav borders and making a sort of "de-nationalized," generic citizen: "The old provincial names were wiped out and the new areas were designated by prominent geographical features. […] Thousands of citizens, previously more conscious of provincial loyalties than of the need for national unity, were brought into government […] Finally, distinctions were obliterated between Serbs, Croats, and Slovenes. All became uniformly Yugoslavs, both politically and before the law." (Kerner, 1949, 127).

With the benefit of hindsight, such a view appears utopian and factually incorrect. King Alexander certainly wished to erase the ethnic identities of his subjects, creating an obliging "Yugoslav" whose only identity derived from physical occupation of an area defined solely by lines drawn on a map and a shared central government. Graham thought that the temporary suppression of ethnic identities meant their action dissolution, but events would prove him terribly wrong in the 1980s and 1990s.

**King Alexander I of Yugoslavia**

At almost the same time the king was asserting his power, Tito busily built his own power using his own arrest and trial as a public venue. In February 1928, he created greater unity within the communist party by calling for an end to factionalism at an important meeting. Becoming the Zagreb Secretary of the Yugoslav Communist Party, Tito leveraged his new position to "advertise" himself, increasing his standing on the global communist scene.

The police first arrested Tito on May Day 1928 when he turned the celebration into a communist demonstration in Zagreb. Released after two weeks in custody, Tito fomented a general strike in response to the June 28th killing of Stjepan Radić, leader of the Croatian Peasant Party. This killing also prompted the dissolution of the constitution by King Alexander and the establishment of the "Kingdom of Yugoslavia" under his personal rule, thus not only bringing Tito to prominence but simultaneously creating the general political structure he would eventually adopt and adapt for his own personal reign.

**Stjepan Radić**

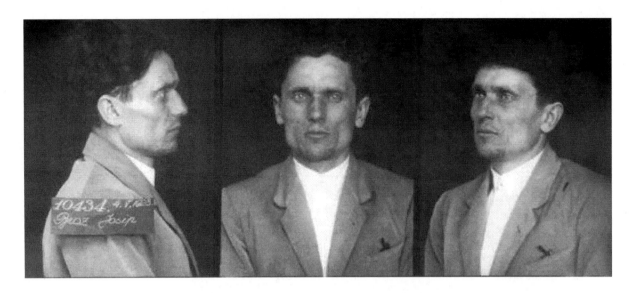

**Tito's mugshot after being arrested**

After starting the strike, Tito attempted to hide from the authorities. Police raiding his apartment found a revolver with ammunition, four hand grenades, and a stack of inflammatory communist propaganda ready for distribution that called for the people to take up arms. When the police found him, Tito gave himself a whiff of the romantic fugitive hero by flourishing a second revolver, though he carefully avoided actually using it.

At the time, Tito claimed that the police planted the grenades and revolver, but once in power, he cheerfully admitted they belonged to him. Tito, recognizing the judicial system as a superb political forum in an era of mass communications, made the most of the situation by ostentatiously starting a hunger strike. This earned him international attention thanks to a communist journal, which published the melodramatically titled piece "A Cry from the Hell of Yugoslavia's Prisons" about Tito's sufferings.

Having gained both national and international attention, Tito – much as Adolf Hitler did in the wake of the Beer Hall Putsch – turned the courtroom into a theater, and his presence there into a piece of "performance art." When told to enter his plea, Tito responded with fine rhetorical flourish: "Although I admit the charges of the state prosecutor's indictment, I do not consider myself guilty because I do not accept the jurisdiction of this bourgeois court. [...] I admit that I am a member of the illegal Yugoslav Communist Party. I admit that I have spread communist ideas and propagated communism, that I have expounded the injustices suffered by the proletariat, in public meetings." (Swain, 2011, 12).

Tito received a five-year sentence, but most of it scarcely represented a serious hardship. Due to his mechanical skill, the prison governor put him in charge of running the jail's electrical generators. With his abilities on display, the prison warders soon allowed him to leave the prison and carry out electrical and mechanical work throughout the town; in effect, for most of his sentence, he lived at the prison but worked outside it.

**Tito and his mentor Moša Pijade in jail**

Released in March 1934, Tito traveled to Moscow in 1935. As he put it, "With what joy I had felt the strength of that country as, emerging from prison in 1934, I listened in the dead of each night to Radio Moscow and heard the clock of the Kremlin tower striking the hours, and the stirring strains of the 'International.'"

Tito headed there because Pelageya had returned to Russia in 1929, after Tito's arrest, taking their son Zarko with her. Filled with communist zeal, she proceeded on to Kazakhstan to teach and to spread the Leninist word, but to Tito's immense astonishment and horror, she had placed

Zarko in an orphanage, and the boy vanished without a trace into the appalling Soviet orphanage system. Tito would not re-establish contact with his son for nine more years, when the young man reappeared in 1944 as a soldier in the Red Army. Tito and Pelageya divorced, and Tito steadfastly refused all her attempts to renew their contact, seemingly still furious over her treatment and losing of Zarko. Stalin's purges did not miss the dedicated communist Pelageya. Sent to prison on some pretext in 1938, she secured her release only 15 years later upon Stalin's death in 1953, after which she lived in Moscow until she died in 1968.

When Tito emerged from prison, Hitler's newly minted Nazi party had achieved power in Germany, quashing the final communist attempts at revolution there. The French communists and fascists continued fighting in Paris and other major cities. The Yugoslav communists now had Milan Gorkic as their leader, appointed by the Comintern. The Comintern weeded out communist leaders they found inadequate with a ruthlessness that echoed the mass "liquidations" of Stalin's 1930s purges. Soon the leading communists grew disillusioned with Milan Gorkic's abilities also.

**Gorkic**

Unwisely, Gorkic obeyed a July 1937 summons to come to Moscow, and when he arrived there, the NKVD arrested him as a British spy, Stalin's favorite category of imagined bugbears. The Russians shot him on November 1st, 1937, and Gorkic's wife soon faced a firing squad also. Out of 900 Yugoslavian communists then in Russia, the secret police arrested 800, of whom only 40 survived.

After that, the Comintern, threatening to cut off their funding of the CPY, gave Tito command over the party, and the Croatian, then in Paris, returned to Yugoslavia to begin his tenure. Before leaving Paris, he took steps to prove his loyalty to Stalin, including the publication of an article proclaiming, "From hidden Trotskyists you often hear: 'I am not a Trotskyist, but neither am I a Stalinist.' Whoever speaks this way is surely a Trotskyist." (Rogovin, 2009, 308).

Tito began working as effective leader of the CPY, attempting to keep the trust of the Comintern while pursuing his own plans as much as he could. Amid the politics of 1930s communism, Tito soon found himself targeted for elimination by the Paris-based Yugoslavian communist Ivan Maric, who began loudly accusing him of being an imitator of Gorkic, and thus, by implication, a follower of Trotsky and a traitor. However, Tito's efforts in Yugoslavia bolstered his case with Comintern. He managed to infiltrate the legal labor unions in Yugoslavia extensively with communist cells. This led to communist control of most of the country's most powerful unions.

Mustering these results as proof of his true communist credentials, Tito boldly traveled to Paris in June 1938, obtained a visa to Moscow, then went on to present his case. Faced by a series of chimeric accusations, Tito hammered on his very real achievements in creating a burgeoning communist worker's movement in Yugoslavia in just a few months. He also received inadvertent help from Maric, who, panicking, wrote to the Comintern saying that he had no objection to Tito and simply wanted several lower-ranking "Gorkicites" purged from the CPY.

The Comintern worked very slowly on its decision, leaving Tito in Moscow for months. Though Tito, in his later writing and interviews, lamented the bloody destruction of Yugoslavian communists during Stalin's purges, an extensive range of documents in Soviet archives reveal that he played the sinister game to the full. Far from watching as a grieved bystander, Tito ruthlessly denounced numerous other Yugoslavians who might rival or oppose him, deliberately working to bring about their execution. He mastered the fevered "anti-Trotskyist" rhetoric of the show trials and worked pitilessly to cause the deaths of dozens of men and women. Tito also effectively announced his intention to drive out his adversaries in a report made in 1939: "The new leadership stands before the task of purging the party of various factionalists and Trotskyist elements both abroad, and in our nation [...] Our party [...] will gladly accept any decision which the Comintern makes." (Rogovin, 2009, 308).

Tito returned to Yugoslavia in early 1939 and proceeded to evict his opponents from the CPY. He opposed a Croatian separatist movement which even the Comintern seemed inclined to endorse. Most of the communists wanted to soothe the Croatians' nationalist feelings, concerned that they would turn to Hitler for assistance in creating a breakaway republic precisely as the Slovaks had in Czechoslovakia that year. Tito, however, pushed for Yugoslavian unity and the creation of a revolutionary republic. The Comintern labeled him a possible Trotskyist and summoned him to Moscow that autumn, a near-certain death sentence, but luck favored the Croatian. The Nazis and Soviets concluded the Molotov-Ribbentrop Pact on August 23rd, 1939, one month before Tito's scheduled Moscow appearance. A week later, Germany invaded Poland on September 1st.

When Tito appeared before the Comintern in Moscow on September 26th, his formerly Trotskyist views had now, in dizzying fashion, become the official party line. Prior to August 23rd, Tito's "left-wing communist" views carried an essentially automatic death sentence in Stalin's regimes. Following the Pact's signing, the exact same views became the official line, while the Comintern's earlier view now received the "counterrevolutionary" label. Sheer random chance had saved Tito from "liquidation" by an NKVD death squad. On November 23rd, the Comintern Secretariat put its seal of approval on Tito's approach to a united Yugoslavia and a "revolutionary republic," and confirmed him solidly as CPY leader. Returning to Yugoslavia in 1940, Tito set to work rapidly to build on this base.

### Ceaușescu's Early Years

"Stealing from capitalism is not like stealing out of our own pockets. Marx and Lenin have taught us that anything is ethical, so long as it is in the interest of the proletarian class and its world revolution." - Nicolae Ceaușescu

Nicolae Ceaușescu was born in the village of Scornicești, in southern Romania around 100 miles to the west of Bucharest, on January 26, 1918. Ceaușescu's family was poor; Nicolae had nine siblings and his parents worked a small plot of land as peasants.

When he was born at the tail end of the First World War, Romania was deeply embroiled in the conflict, and its implications would be felt in the country's development long after 1918. Wedged between the Black Sea, the Western Balkans, and modern-day Ukraine, Romania had been part of the Ottoman Empire until 1877, when the country gained its independence. Initially, Romania had been neutral during the First World War, but in 1916 it had joined France, Russia, and Britain in their fight against Germany, Austria and the Ottomans. The Romanian army, however, performed poorly, which led to Romania being occupied by the Central Powers and forced to sign a humiliating armistice. When Germany was ultimately defeated in November 1918, this agreement was torn up and Romania was granted more territory as a result of the 1919 Treaty of Versailles. Indeed, restoring Romanian sovereignty was the 11th point in American President Woodrow Wilson's famous "Fourteen Points."[1]

---

[1] Brendan Simms, *Europe: The Struggle for Supremacy 1453 to the Present* (London: Penguin, 2014), p. 313.

In the wake of the war, the country was ruled by a monarch, King Ferdinand I, who presided over a "Greater Romania" that incorporated territories such as Transylvania and Bessarabia. Curiously, the royal family could trace their lineage through the Hohenzollern dynasty, which had ruled Prussia (and then Germany) until the end of the war.

**King Ferdinand I**

Despite Romania's apparent success at the end of the conflict, the world that Nicolae Ceaușescu was born into was highly unstable. The entire Balkan region (Romania is sometimes considered to be in the eastern Balkans) was destabilized during the First World War, and the Balkan Wars were a precuros to the bigger conflagration. Territory had changed hands on multiple occasions in most of the constituent countries, populations had been exchanged, and many had seen extreme violence.

Meanwhile, life for peasants such as Ceaușescu's family was usually one of toil and hardship, though The post-1918 regime in Bucharest did initiate some social reforms, such as greater property rights for agricultural small-holders, as well as increased industrial output and exports. Moreover, liberal politicians in the 1920s sought to modernize Romania, and as a result, more jobs were available in larger towns and cities.

Nicolae's father was by all accounts a cruel and abusive man. With only intermittent work and a long-term drinking problem, the elder Ceaușescu has been portrayed by historians as a tyrant.[2] As a result, Nicolae developed into a lonely, frustrated, introverted, and sometimes aggressive adult. At only 11 years old, Nicolae ran away to Bucharest to escape this unhappy situation and took on an apprenticeship as a shoemaker, but cosmopolitan Bucharest was a huge culture shock for Ceaușescu, who struggled to adapt to the city after his upbringing in the countryside. Ceaușescu's sister Niculina took him in as he learned his trade.

Upon entering the world of work, Ceaușescu came under the influence of communists, such as his colleague Alexandru Săndulescu, and in 1932, at the age of 14, Nicolae joined the communist party, which was then banned in Romania. Coming, as he did, from an impoverished family, it is unsurprising that Ceaușescu was taken in by the ideological allure of communism, an ideology that was rising across Europe in the 1920s and 1930s. The 1917 Bolshevik Revolution had shocked the world, and the reverberations were still being felt around Europe. As with many other countries during the era, the ideological certainties of communism and fascism proved highly seductive for many, particularly as economic misery spread.

Politics in Romania had oscillated between similar forces across the rest of Europe. Under the tutelage of the monarch, Romania had moved towards democracy in the 1920s, led by two main parties: the Liberal Party and the National Peasant Party. The latter, led by Iuliu Maniu, won a large majority in the 1928 elections.

---

[2] David Binder, 'The Cult of Ceausescu', *New York Times*, 30 November 1986, https://www.nytimes.com/1986/11/30/magazine/the-cult-of-ceausescu.html, [accessed on 19 November 2018]

**Maniu**

Bucharest had aimed to maintain security through alliances such as the 1924 "Little Entente" agreement with Yugoslavia and Czechoslovakia, as well as maintaining cordial relations with the major powers, committed to democratic countries across Europe. Still, as with so many of its contemporaries, authoritarian forces lurked close to the surface of Romanian politics, and they were ready to break out into the open after the 1929 Wall Street Crash and subsequent Great Depression. Economic decline acted as a catalyst for a number of groups, most notably far-right nationalists, anti-Semites, religious groups, and communists. The Romanian Communist Party had been banned in 1924, and it still remained formally under the command of the Soviets back in Moscow.

King Carol II took the throne in 1930, right as a major economic crisis descended upon Romania. He was deeply authoritarian, and his outlook would cast a shadow over the country in the 1930s, thanks to rhetoric that could be exploited by others in later years. He created a personality cult around himself and purported to speak for the common man against the corrupt elites represented by the main political parties. He also pandered to anti-Semitic sentiment in Romanian society. Therefore, as a result of external economic events and geopolitical uncertainty and insecurity, coupled with a shift to populism and the move towards political extremes at home, Romania entered a troubled period.

**King Carol II**

It was against this political backdrop that Ceaușescu had joined the Communist Party. Membership of the communists meant a life (or at least a double life) underground and out of sight of the authorities, but Ceaușescu would attend clandestine meetings and was an enthusiastic follower of communist teachings. Despite the furtive efforts, he soon came to the attention of the authorities in the increasingly stifling environment of the 1930s, leading to his exile back to his home town. In short order, he would sneak back into Bucharest.

The Romanian authorities became increasingly concerned about communist activities during the 1930s, and many faced stiff penalties if discovered to be part of the movement. Ceaușescu himself was jailed in 1936 for his communist sympathies and street violence, but that actually allowed him to make contacts with people who would prove crucial in his subsequent political rise, most notably communist leader Gheorghe Gheorghiu-Dej.

**Ceauşescu in 1936**

**Gheorghe Gheorghiu-Dej**

### World War II

"The peoples of Yugoslavia do not want Fascism. They do not want a totalitarian regime, they do not want to become slaves of the German and Italian financial oligarchy as they never wanted to become reconciled to the semi-colonial dependence imposed on them by the so-called Western democracies after the first imperialist war." - Tito

Over the course of 1940, Tito swiftly expanded Communist Party of Yugoslavia membership, taking it from 1,500 to 8,000 members. Though still officially illegal, the CPY did achieve some measure of respectability when the older, failing, legal parties applied to it for help and advice. A communique authored by the CPY openly declared its intention to found a communist republic created from a broad-based revolution: "We communists consider that in this final hour it is essential to unite all those forces which are ready to struggle [...] however, we communists further consider that such militant unity will only really bring results when it is achieved not only between leaders but from below, among the depths of the working masses." (Swain, 2011, 29).

Tito sensed that the Germans might eventually invade Yugoslavia, anticipating this event as an opportunity. He planned for strong communist partisan forces to retreat to the mountains, while leaving agents behind in the towns. When the Germans eventually weakened, he thought, the partisans could sweep out of their montane fastnesses and conquer Yugoslavia in the name of

Leninist revolution.

In fact, Tito had scarcely laid his plans before Hitler's panzer divisions roared over the Yugoslavian border. Ostensibly assisting the Croatians in their bid for independence, the Wehrmacht invaded on April 6th, 1941. With typical German speed, the 2nd and 12th Armies crashed through the Yugoslavian defenses, seizing the capital Belgrade by April 13th. The Royal Yugoslav Army surrendered on April 17th, ending official resistance.

In the wake of the Nazi conquest, the old divisions the monarchy attempted to paper over burst out afresh, perhaps strengthened and exaggerated by their brief suppression. The Croatians established the Independent State of Croatia, a curious mix of puppet state and independent ally on the side of the Germans. Intense partisan warfare soon began, launched by the Ustashe, an alliance of Catholic Croatians and Bosniak Muslims determined to drive out or eradicate the Serbs. Even the Germans found themselves somewhat taken aback at the extent of the massacres and violence committed by the Ustashe, with Edmund Glaise-Horstenau reporting that "according to reliable reports from countless German military and civilian observers during the last few weeks, in country and town, the Ustasha have gone raging mad." (West, 1994, 98).

Glaise-Horstenau initially attempted to protect the Serbs to some extent, but with only six battalions of Wehrmacht at his disposal, he could but stop just a small fraction of the violence. This, in turn, kindled an answering aggression in the Serbs, a pugnacious, defiant people throughout all of their history. Soon the Serbian Chetniks opposed the Ustashe, while collaborating to a considerable degree with the Axis forces in many areas. Ante Pavelic, head of the new Croatian state, assured Glaise-Horstenau repeatedly that he would rein in the Ustashe but never did so.

**Pavelic and Hitler**

Tito proved reluctant to seize the opportunity to become leader of the communist Partisan movement. He had married Herta Haas, his second wife, and did not wish to leave her and his new son. However, by May, events forced him to flee to Belgrade, where the communist leadership had already gone. Tito issued several proclamations, including an upbeat revolutionary document vowing that Yugoslavia would rise and throw off the occupier's yoke in a communist revolution. The killings by the Ustashe, otherwise known as the Black Legion, won him many Serbian recruits, as did oppressive Germanic rule. The various factions quickly mushroomed into armies; by the end of 1941, the Partisans already numbered 80,000 men and women, while the Chetniks fielded 20,000 and the Ustashe 16,000 supplemented by a powerful "Home Guard" of 85,000. All sides would eventually organize their forces into divisions as their numbers continued expanding.

Tito received the post of Commander-in-Chief of the National Liberation Army of Yugoslavia on June 27th, 1941, by decree of the Politboro of the Central Committee of the CPY. Wielding his new authority, Tito began operations almost immediately in Serbia proper. A region of forested hills and tough, fierce people, Serbia seemed an excellent starting point for establishing a Partisan base area. As Tito explained, "While looking over the configuration of the terrains of Serbia, I saw that western Serbia was most suitable for us, for the orientation of our fighting units, for the organisation of our partisan units and for the creation of a certain free territory […]

at the beginning we did not believe that we would create a large free territory so soon." (Swain, 2011, 35).

In fact, thanks to large numbers of Wehrmacht troops being withdrawn for participation in Operation Barbarossa, the invasion of the Soviet Union, Tito's initial plan experienced unexpected success. In August and September of 1941, the Partisans managed to seize most of Serbia, enabling Tito to relocate his headquarters to Uzice. A separate July uprising in Montenegro by the region's inhabitants, who lived up to the death-defying reputation their people had won over the centuries, ousted the Italians from much of Montenegro.

The Partisans' success in resisting the Germans and other factions came both from the intense fighting spirit and courage of all the Yugoslav ethnicities and their large stocks of weapons. Sporting and hunting rifles abounded in prewar Yugoslavia, enabling the partisans of all stripes to attack paramilitary and military posts, thereby obtaining further large caches of weapons in the process. Deserting Yugoslav army soldiers also supplied rifles, pistols, hand grenades, machine guns, and ammunition.

On September 19th, Tito met with Chetnik leader Dragoljub Mihailovic, known to his men as "Uncle Draza," a bearded, bespectacled man who would soon become Tito's bitter enemy. The two leaders formed a temporary alliance for the purpose of expanding the "free territory" already won. Tito wanted to go vigorously on the offensive, while Mihailovic urged a more cautious approach to avoid reprisals.

**Mihailovic**

Galled by the remarkable successes of the Partisans and resistance by numerous small bands of armed men loosely affiliated or unaffiliated with the major movements, the Germans launched the First Anti-Partisan Offensive on September 20th. The Chetniks attacked the Partisans at the same time as they fought the Germans, despite attempts by Tito and Mihailovic to negotiate a truce. The Serbians felt deep and not entirely unwarranted alarm by the fact that the Partisans enforced a monopoly of communist government in Western Serbia, suppressing other parties despite their strong support.

Two German divisions, strengthened by elements of four more and bolstered by two volunteer Serbian units, eventually threw the Partisans and Chetniks out of western Serbia, recapturing Uzice in the process. Tito himself barely escaped, leaving his headquarters, submachine gun in hand, just 20 minutes before German *Landsers* reached it. Remarking on this event, Tito admitted that "we did not think that the Germans would go through the liberated territory like a knife through butter, we expected steady pressure and that we would be able to hold on for a long time, that we would get more organised and produce more arms." (Swain, 2011, 41).

Tito offered his resignation to the Politboro in case they wanted to hold him responsible for the disaster, but he found himself left in command nevertheless. Mihailovic continued fighting the Germans also, though he observed that Tito's open resistance had indeed triggered several reprisal massacres by the Germans.

During 1942 and 1943, a seesaw battle moved back and forth across the landscape of Yugoslavia, as first the Germans and then the Partisans gained the upper hand. The gleeful ferocity of the Partisans often matched or exceeded that of their opponents, and the British intelligence officers attached to the Yugoslavian forces often found themselves stunned by the bloodthirsty relentlessness and outright cruelty of both their allies and foes. The intense resistance in Yugoslavia troubled the Axis leaders, Mussolini in particular. At the very end 1941, the Duce wrote to the Fuhrer, "Balkans. It is necessary to eliminate all the hotbeds of insurrection before spring. They might cause the broadening of the war in the Balkans. We should pacify Bosnia first, then Serbia and Montenegro. It is necessary for our armed forces to collaborate according to a common plan, in order to avoid a loss of energy and to reach the desired results with the least amount of men and material." (Dedijer, 1953, 184),

Hitler accepted this proposal, and the anti-partisan actions in Yugoslavia developed almost precisely as Mussolini laid out. The Second Anti-Partisan Offensive began in January 1942 and continued through February, evicting the Partisans from Eastern Serbia. The follow-up operation, the Third Anti-Partisan Offensive, aimed not only at Serbia but also at Bosnia, Herzegovina, and Montenegro. During the Third Partisan Offensive, the Germans, Italians, Ustashe, and those Chetniks who now openly cooperated with the invaders in anti-Partisan operations pushed forward slowly against heavy resistance in March 1942. The protracted offensive continued throughout April and into early May.

On May 1st, Tito held the Partisan Olympics at Foca. With the Commander-in-Chief as a spectator, teams from the Supreme HQ, First Proletarian Brigade, and assorted other units contended at volleyball, soccer, and field and track. At this point, the leading Italian units continued their advance just 7 miles distant. After the Olympics, Tito withdrew his five Proletarian Brigades into the mountains between Bosnia and Montenegro, eluding an Axis encirclement attempt. At one point, Tito came across a small abandoned mill and, overtaken by his old obsession, worked for 30 minutes on the mill machinery. Once the mill started working again, Tito and his men moved on.

From there, the Proletarian Brigades and other Partisan units launched a counteroffensive in Eastern Bosnia. Tito liberated the regional capital Bihac, along with 10 other towns, with 30,000 Partisans installed as a garrison force. Though the Partisans endured numerous hardships campaigning in the rough terrain and wild countryside, they maintained a high esprit de corps, as one account suggests: "After two days of battle, we were tired, dirty and hungry. Passing through a town, the people there ran out onto the streets to wave at and greet us. The battalion commander told one soldier with a strong voice to lead the troops in a song. They sang with him, loudly and clearly. We raised our heads, our exhaustion disappeared and each step became stronger and more resolute. The people watched us and admired us. They said, "There goes the people's army, the Proletarians." (Vuksic, 2003, 31).

The Germans called this liberated area "Tito's Territory," clearly recognizing the figurehead and mastermind behind the massively successful Partisan movement. Tito, though a communist and therefore officially an atheist, ordered his men to restore the Serbian churches dismantled or decommissioned by the Ustashe. This won him immense popularity among the masses of ordinary Serbs, who provided him with hundreds of thousands of fearlessly aggressive infantry. By late 1942, Tito's Partisans mustered so many men and women that a larger unit – the Corps, consisting of 9 divisions – appeared in the organizational table of the growing army. The Partisans had almost reached the organization and professionalism of a regular army, though they proved just as apt to commit massacres as the Ustashe.

In the beginning of 1943, the Germans and Italians under General Alexander von Leer launched the Fourth Anti-Partisan Offensive, also known as Operation White (*Fall Weiss*). 90,000 men supported by 12 air squadrons participated in the offensive. These included the 7th SS Volunteer Mountain Division *Prinz Eugen* under SS-Gruppenfuhrer Artur Gustav Phleps, and the 369th (Croatian) Infantry Division, known as the "Devil's Division" (Teufels-Division), among others. Marking the unusual nature of the Yugoslavian war, the Chetniks fought alongside the Italians – as allies, rather than servants or collaborators – yet retained a deadly enmity with the Germans. While the Chetniks attacked the communist Partisans, they remained prepared to attack the Germans also, while the German High Command ordered their troops to wipe out the Chetniks if they came in contact with them.

This bizarre mix of enmity and alliance did not flow in only one direction. Tito opened negotiations with the Germans for a time in March, and during that interval, he issued an order to his troops: "On your way, do not fight Germans [...] Your most important task at this moment is to annihilate the Chetniks of Draza Mihailovic and to destroy their command apparatus which represents the greatest danger to the development of the National Liberation Struggle."(Roberts, 1987, 102).

With his characteristic audacity and initiative, Tito turned the Fourth Anti-Partisan Offensive into a springboard for a Partisan offensive into Montenegro. The Partisans seized most of Montenegro and smashed the Chetniks as a military force, after which the Germans mopped up their remnants and nearly managed to capture or kill Mihailovic.

1943 witnessed two more offensives against Tito's forces. The Fifth Anti-Partisan Offensive struck at Tito's new "free territories" in Montenegro, using 117,000 men supported by over 300 combat aircraft. Heavy fighting continued for months, during which the Germans killed 7,543 Partisan combatants, suffering 913 KIA and 2,132 MIA (probably KIA, given the universal tendency to take no prisoners). This offensive, Operation Black, nevertheless failed, leaving the Partisans in control of Montenegro.

**Tito and Ivan Ribar in 1943**

The Sixth Offensive occurred in the east towards the end of the year, aiming at Bosnia. Consisting of Operation Kugelblitz and Operation Schneesturm (Ball Lightning and Snowstorm), the offensive inflicted heavy losses on the Partisans but failed to break up the structure of their units, thus proving largely futile.

During the harsh fighting in Yugoslavia, Tito developed his own set of military rules, designed to amplify the strengths of his irregular Partisan forces. He always ordered the utmost efforts to be given to care for the wounded. In the event of an enemy offensive, safe evacuation of the wounded took top priority, and, in fact, formed the focus of several major battles during the Fourth and Fifth Offensives. Tito believed this increased the morale of his men, and considering the daring and courage often showed by his Partisans, reality seemingly bore out the concept's validity.

Tito also worked hard to inculcate his soldiers with the idea that being surrounded did not mean their doom. Instead, the Partisans received training to pick a single spot in encircling troops and throw their full weight against it vigorously. This almost always permitted a successful breakout even against superior numbers.

Two other precepts of "Tito-style warfare" included the necessity for officers to undergo the same risks as ordinary soldiers, thus preventing resentment, and rear area spoiling attacks during enemy advances. Any major forward thrust by German, Italian, or Ustashe forces triggered deployment of numerous Partisan raiding parties, who infiltrated the rear of the advancing force. These men and women then did their best to disrupt hostile communications to the utmost, making the advance more difficult and less coordinated.

With the Allies in Italy, just across the Adriatic, and an invasion of Normandy looming (though the extensive British deception plan made the Germans believe Calais the main target), the Germans made a desperate but well-planned effort to eliminate the guiding spirit of the Partisans – Tito himself – in 1944. The year opened with Tito executing another of his key maneuvers – when pushed out of one area by an Axis offensive, immediately and simultaneously launching an offensive into a fresh area to gain new territory. As he described this method, "[W]e must not let the enemy force us by clever tactics onto the defensive. We must make up for the loss of one area by the conquest of a larger and more important area." (Greentree, 2012, 13-14).

**Tito and the Partisan Supreme Command in May 1944**

This time, however, the Germans clearly identified Tito's strategy. The Abwehr deployed 10 FAT (Frontaufklärungstruppe) intelligence teams, who developed a network of local agents to pin down Tito's location. Finally, the Germans deployed an elite unit of Brandenburger Commandos known as the Benesch Special Unit to track the elusive Partisan Commander-in-Chief down. Disguising themselves as farmers and partisans, these men infiltrated the region where intelligence suggested Tito might be found, near the town of Drvar in a valley of the Dinaric Alps. These daring men, knowing certain death awaited them if captured out of uniform, infiltrated among the equally daring Partisans.

To the particular alarm of Tito's lieutenants, they uncovered and captured a German agent within the Partisan leader's headquarters staff in March 1944. Worse, from their viewpoint, the German managed to escape from the cell where he awaited execution and vanished into the countryside. Tito began using one alpine cave as his HQ and sleeping in another to make his location harder to pin down.

Eventually, the Germans decided to send in a unique unit to kill Tito, the 500th SS Parachute Battalion. Formed mainly of SS men who had been sentenced to a special detention camp for minor disciplinary infractions, the Battalion also included a range of volunteers. These men received training in parachute and glider operations, and soon numbered 1,140, organized into 5 companies. The operation, dubbed Operation Rösselsprung or Knight's Move (a chess term), involved dropping the 500th SS Parachute Battalion directly in the valley near Drvar, following a preparatory Stuka dive-bombing attack. Simultaneously, five motorized columns would converge on the suspected location of Tito's headquarters. Several dozen DFS 230 gliders would provide the means for the 500th's airborne assault.

Tito should have been at Bastasi when the attack came on May 25th, 1944, but he had remained at Drvar due to the fact he celebrated his birthday on that date (rather than the actual date of May 7th). Tito's cave headquarters represented a well-appointed lodging, as a description underlines: "In a natural cleft in the rock three flights of wooden steps led to [...] a natural cave, inside which rooms had been constructed with a veranda in front commanding a fine view across the valley. Great wooden beams supported the construction and inside in Tito's office the walls were lined, and the windows curtained with parachute silk, while a huge British military map of Yugoslavia covered a wall behind his desk." (Greentree, 2012, 30).

Just after sunrise on May 25th, 14 Stuka dive-bombers and a squadron of Italian light bombers attacked suspected Partisan positions in and around Drvar. Immediately after the bombing, a wave of paratroopers from the 500th SS Parachute Battalion landed, followed by the main force in gliders. The Germans landed in a wide arc around Drvar, often very close to their objectives, while more landed on the heights above the town to seal off escape into the forested mountains. A ferocious firefight erupted at the Communist Party Central Committee headquarters, which the Germans mistook for a communications center. The SS men cleared the building after a lethal gun-battle.

The Germans, working efficiently, cleared Drvar of resistance by 9 AM, taking a high number of prisoners. At this point, three captured CV-35 tanks – light Italian designs – counterattacked the Germans with their machine guns. The Germans had no antitank weapons available to counter these small vehicles, which pinned them down for several minutes. SS Oberscharführer Hummel ran to one of the tanks and blocked its vision slit with his camouflage smock. However, a 16-year-old female Partisan, Mika Bosnic, rushed to the tank, and, before the Germans shot her, pulled the smock clear. The tanks soon retreated, presumably having exhausted their machine gun ammunition.

One of the prisoners almost immediately revealed the location of Tito's cave, pointing reflexively to its location when a German showed him the Partisan leader's photograph. Tito soon observed German soldiers closing on the cave across the valley floor. SS machine gun teams set up heavy machine guns, sited to prevent anyone from leaving the cave mouth alive.

Tito, along with the 12 men and 8 women in the cave with him, escaped through the floor. Cutting through the floorboards, they lowered a rope ladder into the stream flowing under part of the HQ, Thick vegetation hid the streambed from observation, and the partisans had earlier placed a rope ladder up the cleft of the falling stream to the plateau above. Tito, his followers, and his Alsatian dog Tiger climbed up to safety. As Tito put it, "I left with the help of my escort and my dog, Tiger. After we climbed for a while, I had to take a rest. Tiger came to me. He started to whine. I grabbed him by the snout to keep him quiet. There were times that I thought we would have to shoot him with a pistol, because he would betray us, but I couldn't bring myself to do it." (Greentree, 2012, 52-53).

With Tito clear, the Partisans mounted increasingly powerful counterattacks against the 500th SS Parachute Battalion, forcing it back into a defensive perimeter. The Germans held out overnight despite constant heavy attacks, with the Partisans drawing off at morning when Luftwaffe air support arrived. Later on May 26th, the German motorized forces arrived, including the feared 7th SS Division "Prinz Eugen." After some additional fighting, the Partisans retreated, as a German officer recounted: "We stormed up the hill and in a single rush, firing from the hip and lobbing hand grenades, we crushed the enemy. The entire regiment [...] pursued the enemy as he fled to the north. The latter offered no resistance, because their objective of enabling Tito to escape had been achieved. Tito got away, though [...] he had to leave his brand new Marshal's uniform behind." (Kurowski, 2005, 269).

After his escape, Tito allowed the Allies to evacuate him, first by air and then by sea, to the island of Vis in the Adriatic. There he set up his headquarters in another cave. The Germans soon located him there, but the island's defenses proved so formidable that they made no further attempts on the Partisan leader there.

At this moment, politics entered the picture amid the continuing military operations. British Prime Minister Winston Churchill sent Ivan Subasic to Vis, compelling Tito, using the lever of British aid, to nominally accept the legitimacy of King Petar, currently in exile in England. Tito felt rather displeased at this, preferring not to have any dealings with the monarchy due to his communist leanings. Nonetheless, Tito traveled to confer with Winston Churchill in Naples on August 12th. At the meeting, the Partisan leader promised to allow a multi-party democracy in Yugoslavia, essentially promising the Englishman whatever he wanted as long as Allied support for the Yugoslavian Partisans continued.

**Tito and Churchill in Italy in 1944**

On the night of September 18th to 19th, 1944, Tito slipped off Vis on a journey to Moscow, which he did not warn the British about. In Moscow, he met with Stalin, and Tito took a surprisingly independent tone in his conference with the Soviet strongman, essentially stating that if the Soviets did not assist him, they should at least stand out of his way. Hearing Tito still complaining about King Petar, Stalin offered some avuncular counsel: "You don't have to return him forever. Only for a while, then slip a knife into his back at the opportune moment." (Banac, 1988, 14).

Stalin and Tito agreed that the Soviets would take Belgrade and leave the rest of Yugoslavia's liberation to the Partisans, which is exactly what happened. Except for a Soviet incursion as far as Belgrade, the now gigantic, 800,000-strong Partisan army swept forward on a last offensive in late 1944 and into 1945. Carrying all resistance before them, the Yugoslavian forces smashed the last resistance by May 15th, 1945, a week after V-E Day marked Germany's unconditional surrender. Tito would say of the war, "Our sacrifices are terrible. I can safely say that there is no other part of the world which has been devastated on a vaster scale than Yugoslavia. Every tenth Yugoslav has perished in this struggle in which we were forced to wrest armaments from our enemies, to freeze without clothing, and to die without medication. Nevertheless our optimism and faith have proved justified. The greatest gain of this conflict between democracy and fascism lies in the fact that it has drawn together everything that was good in humanity. The unity of the United States, the Soviet Union and Great Britain is the best guarantee to the peoples of the world that Nazi horrors will never again be repeated."

**A celebration held for Tito near the end of the war**

**World War II in Romania**

Throughout the 1930s, Romania was being drawn into the troubles of continental Europe. As with so many other European countries, Romania experienced social and civil unrest, support for extreme parties and numerous unstable governments, and by 1938 the country effectively became a dictatorship under King Carol II. This was a trend that had been seen in Yugoslavia and Bulgaria, but those authoritarian regimes would easily fall prey to the overtures of Nazi

Germany and Soviet Russia. Out of the turmoil of the 1930s and 1940s, a very different Romania would emerge, with the unlikely figure of Ceaușescu close to the corridors of power.

Romania had again attempted to stay neutral as war broke out in 1939, but it was obviously in an extremely hostile neighbourhood. After several months of inaction between the major powers in 1939 and early 1940, Nazi Germany made rapid inroads on the Western front and by mid-1940 controlled much of continental Europe. Far right nationalism and fascism had supporters in Romania, and one of the major groups was called the "Iron Guard," which urged King Carol II to join forces with the Axis.

As Hitler and Mussolini negotiated with other Eastern European countries to join them in 1940, a number of claims were made on the territory Romania had acquired in 1919. As a result, Romanian influence on lands now controlled by the Nazis was diminished, leading to a coup and King Carol II being forced from power.

The king was replaced by Ion Antonescu, who ruled Romania in an authoritarian manner. Antonescu committed the Romanian army to the Second World War, including the Nazi invasion of the Soviet Union. Antonescu was deeply implicated in the Holocaust, and it was subsequently reported that up to 380,000 Jews were murdered in Romanian territory during the war.[3]

---

[3] International Commission on the Holocaust in Romania, "Executive Summary: Historical Findings and Recommendations". *Final Report of the International Commission on the Holocaust in Romania*. Yad Vashem (The Holocaust Martyrs' and Heroes' Remembrance Authority), 11 November 2004.

**Antonescu**

In August 1944, the Soviet Red Army moved into Romania and King Michael I staged a coup in Bucharest, switching his country's allegiance from the Axis to the Allies. The Romanian army then took part in the final offensives to defeat Nazi Germany as the Wehrmacht was pushed back towards its own borders.

**King Michael I**

Peace finally came to Europe in May 1945, but by then half a million Romanians had died as a result of the conflict. Romania was not punished as severely as others after the war ended in 1945, although it was forced to pay reparations to the USSR of $300 million.[4] In the aftermath of a ceasefire, Romania was occupied by the Red Army, in a similar fashion to other countries in Central Europe and Eastern Europe. The Soviets were imposing a buffer zone between non-communist countries that it felt could prove potentially hostile, and the occupation authorities used their position to encourage, and often impose, communist politics in the region. Romania would be no different.

During World War II, Ceaușescu spent several years in prison, which took their toll on him

---

[4] Misha Glenny, *The Balkans 1804-2012: Nationalism, War and the Great Powers* (London: Granta, 2012), p. 521.

physically while hardening him mentally. Serving time in the notorious Doftana Prison in Brasov, Ceaușescu is said to have been beaten so severely that he was left with a stutter for the remainder of his life.[5] He was in and out of prison frequently in the first year of the war, but after the fascists held sway in 1940, the dictatorship jailed him for his longest stint behind bars. This also included time in an internment camp.

**A 1943 picture of Ceaușescu (second from left) in a concentration camp**

[5] Ralph Blumenthal, 'Upheaval in the East: Obituary - The Ceaușescus: 24 Years of Fierce Repression, Isolation and Independence', *New York Times*, 26 December 1989, https://www.nytimes.com/1989/12/26/obituaries/upheaval-east-obituary-Ceaușescus-24-years-fierce-repression-isolation.html, [accessed 7 November 2018]

**A 1944 picture of Ceaușescu at a public meeting**

It was during this time that, alongside Gheorghiu-Dej once more, Ceaușescu was given a more comprehensive training in Marxist-Leninist theory.[6] It is believed that Ceaușescu impressed Gheorghiu-Dej during prison "self-criticism" sessions whereby prisoners tested their commitment to communist ideals.

In the chaos of August 1944, as Romania was invaded and switched sides, Gheorghiu-Dej and Ceaușescu - with the assistance of lawyer Ion Gheorghe Maurer - escaped from prison. Ceaușescu served as Secretary of the Youth Section of the Union of Communists in the final year of the conflict.

**The Rise of Communism in Romania**

"The solving of domestic problems belongs exclusively to the Party and people of each country and any kind of interference can only do harm to the cause of socialism, friendship and collaboration among the socialist countries." - Ceaușescu

After the war, the Russian occupiers were looking for sympathetic Romanians to promote,

---

[6] Ibid.

preferably ones who had not been tainted by the previous regimes. In essence, Ceaușescu was exactly the kind of communist they were looking to recruit. Young, aggressively pro-communism and anti-fascist, fluent in Marxist-Leninism, and with the credibility of having served time for his beliefs, Ceaușescu represented a model candidate for the Communist Central Committee in 1945, and the Soviet authorities assigned him to the political directorate of the Romanian army as a Brigadier General.[7]

Despite the significant communist activity of the 1930s, prominent party member Ana Pauker, who had been exiled in Moscow, returned to Romania after the war to find only about 1,000 other members in the whole of Romania.[8] However, by 1948 this figure had risen to 200,000.[9]

**Pauker**

Ceaușescu also found time to marry a communist party member in 1947. He had met Elena Petrescu in the late 1930s during a period of freedom from prison when they both attended a communist meeting. They would form a strong bond and stay in contact over the following years

[7] Ralph Blumenthal, 'Upheaval in the East: Obituary - The Ceaușescus: 24 Years of Fierce Repression, Isolation and Independence', *New York Times*, 26 December 1989, https://www.nytimes.com/1989/12/26/obituaries/upheaval-east-obituary-Ceaușescus-24-years-fierce-repression-isolation.html, [accessed 7 November 2018]

[8] Misha Glenny, *The Balkans 1804-2012: Nationalism, War and the Great Powers* (London: Granta, 2012), p. 521.

[9] Ibid, p. 521.

until marrying almost 10 years later.

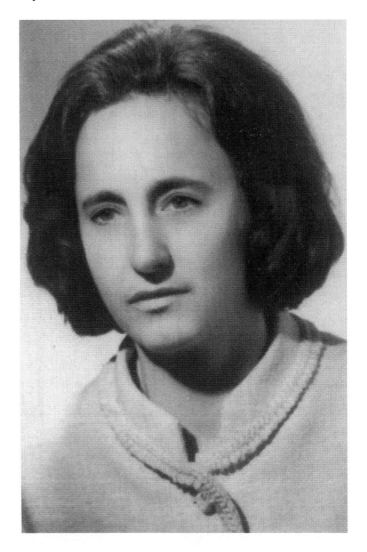

**Elena**

As Ceaușescu began his rise, Romanian politics broadly split into two factions after 1945. There were monarchists loyal to King Michael and proto-democrats or anti-monarchists, themselves divided into pre-war parties such as the National Peasant's Party (NPP) and the communists supported by the Soviets.

As occupiers, the Soviets could obviously promote the latter, and this was evident in elections held in November 1946, where the Soviet-backed communists under the guise of the "Bloc of Democratic Parties" (BDP) won a huge victory with 84% of the vote. As that total suggests, there was evidence of widespread electoral fraud and rigging of votes. After that, the communists then sought to sideline more moderate parties such as the NPP, and a number of show trials led to the convictions and executions of prominent NPP figures and Nazi collaborators, including Antonescu. Ceaușescu himself took charge of the Ministry of Agriculture, a remarkable elevation for someone still under 30 years old and who had little experience with positions of responsibility.

At this time, the two most powerful communist politicians were Gheorghiu-Dej and Dr. Petru Groza, who had been Prime Minister since 1945. Gheorghiu-Dej and Groza forced King Michael to abdicate in December 1947 and soon proclaimed the People's Republic of Romania. Within the space of a few months, a new constitution had been signed and other political parties were forced to merge with the communists or outlawed. In almost no time at all, Romania had been transformed into an authoritarian, communist, one-party state, and opponents were exiled or jailed. Similar techniques were employed in other nearby countries, including Poland, Hungary, East Germany, Yugoslavia, and Czechoslovakia. Romania now sat amongst a bloc of communist states allied to the Soviet Union, and it would not emerge from this political situation for another 40 years. Naturally, Ceauşescu welcomed this chain of events, and his alliance with Gheorghiu-Dej would put him a strong position as the communist system was solidified in the 1950s.

**Groza**

Romanian communists initiated a familiar tranche of policies after they took complete power of the state in 1948. These included the nationalization of virtually all businesses and enterprises that summer, and persecution of any dissenting voices. In most respects, the Romanian communist regime can be considered extremely repressive, suffocating and amongst the most authoritarian of the Cold War. On the other hand, Romania has also been put into a separate basket of communist regimes, sharing some similarities with Tito's Yugoslavia, in so far as it sometimes took a different, more idiosyncratic and independent path that brought it into conflict with Moscow.

One of the foundational events related to the latter trend was the 1948 Tito-Stalin split. In 1947, Stalin had brought together communist regimes and parties under the *Cominform* (the international Communist Information Bureau), headquartered in Belgrade. Tito, however, had enraged Stalin by pursuing an independent foreign policy and ignoring Moscow's set strategy. As a result, Yugoslavia was expelled from the *Cominform* in June 1948 and its offices moved to the Romanian capital of Bucharest.[10]

Romania always managed to remain under Moscow's umbrella despite some precarious moments, but in 1948, Stalinism was very much the communist model of choice. Among the Stalinists, there emerged three factions, including one led by Ana Pauker and a separate group with Gheorghiu-Dej as the dominant figure. The Soviet leader himself supported Gheorghiu-Dej, helping him consolidate his power between the late 1940s and 1952. Gheorghiu-Dej was able to exploit Stalin's anti-Semitic prejudice, as Pauker was Jewish.[11] He then purged his opponents from positions of influence, installing his own supporters.

Gheorghiu-Dej was a wholehearted disciple of Stalin and used the Soviet leader's techniques of show trials in disposing of his enemies, as well as deterring future rivals. A historian of the Balkans, Misha Glenny, described Gheorghiu-Dej as the "worst thug" of all the "little Stalin's" who emerged in the region after the war.[12] If anything, the Romanian communist sought to achieve a prime position in Stalin's eyes through the ferocity of his suppression measures, particularly after the split with Tito.[13] In the process, Gheorghiu-Dej persecuted and imprisoned several groups in apparent waves of oppression. First, he focused on the agricultural peasants, and then he moved against businessmen and religious leaders. The Romanian regime also used "volunteers" - political prisoners in the form of slave labor - to build infrastructure and for other public works projects in the 1950s.

Gheorghiu-Dej was also intent on modernizing Romania through industrialization and urban

---

[10] 'Gorbachev Faults Stalin on Rift With Tito', *The New York Times* 17 March 1988, https://www.nytimes.com/1988/03/17/world/gorbachev-faults-stalin-on-rift-with-tito.html, [accessed 8 November 2018]

[11] Misha Glenny, *The Balkans 1804-2012: Nationalism, War and the Great Powers* (London: Granta, 2012), p. 553.

[12] Ibid, p. 552.

[13] Ibid, p. 553.

development. Gheorghiu-Dej's vision of a communist Romania was of a piece with Stalin's 1930s strategy, which actually brought the Romanian communist leader into conflict with Nikita Khrushchev after Stalin's death in 1953. Khrushchev proposed that Romania supply the communist world with much of its agricultural produce. This plan, a veritable division of labour in the Adam Smith tradition but with a centrally-planned flavour, was rigorously rejected by Gheorghiu-Dej, still focused on his industrialization strategy.

**Khrushchev**

Ceaușescu achieved rapid personal advancement under Gheorghiu-Dej. From heading the young communists at the end of the war to working in the Ministry of Agriculture, as well as a deputy position in the Ministry of Defence, Ceaușescu had utilized the relationship he developed with Gheorghiu-Dej during his wartime imprisonment. Despite having only limited formal education, Ceaușescu proved to be a highly effective bureaucrat and manager. He was said to be intelligent and capable, but also cunning and ruthless. This combination of attributes helped him, along with Gheorghiu-Dej's sponsorship, rise quickly among the communist ranks.

When Gheorghiu-Dej finally purged Ana Pauker and her faction in 1952, he brought Ceaușescu into the Central Committee. Pauker, who had served as Romanian Foreign Minister between 1947-1952, was arrested and subjected to imprisonment and a show trial, only to be released after Stalin's death. She was forced to retire and was politically inactive until her death in 1960. Ceaușescu, however, continued his rise, and in 1954 he became a full member of the all-powerful Politburo.

### Tito's Yugoslavia

"Comrade Khrushchev often repeats that Socialism cannot be built with American wheat. I think it can be done by anyone who knows how to do it, while a person who doesn't know how to do it cannot build Socialism even with his own wheat. Khrushchev says we live on charity received from the imperialist countries … What moral right have those who attack us to rebuke us about American aid or credits when Khruschev himself has just tried to conclude an economic agreement with America?" - Tito

Following the end of World War II, the Yugoslav Army (formerly the Partisans) executed tens of thousands of their adversaries, including former Chetniks, Ustashe, and others. Mihailovic himself fell into Yugoslavian hands, and the Yugoslavs executed him in 1946. This, of course, also had the fringe benefit of eliminating many people who might have objected strenuously to the establishment of a communist state.

Tito, riding a wave of triumph and military glory, brazenly engineered the takeover of the nation by his party, the People's Front, in late 1945. Though Yugoslavia held elections on November 27th, 1945, Tito loaded the ballot-boxes in his favor by declaring that large lists of people could not vote due to supposed collaboration with the Germans. In fact, the list consisted mostly of people believed to be anti-communist, with no reference in most cases to any real connection with the Germans.

Since he had effectively declared that only Partisans and their known supporters could vote, Tito engineered a 90% victory for the People's Front. With his party now immovably in power, Tito abolished the monarchy just two days after the general election, and King Petar II Karadjordjevic fled to the United States, where he died in 1970.

**King Petar II**

Initially, Yugoslavia showed itself to be a ferociously Marxist state, with a secret police, purges of dissenters, numerous arrests, and suppression of religion in the name of communist atheism. Catholic Archbishop Alois Stepinac received a prison sentence of 16 years for alleged

Ustashe activity, though the communists steadily reduced his sentence later. The Archbishop's imprisonment caused the Pope to excommunicate Tito.

Tito's communist party also took over most of the major industries immediately. Tito launched a Five-Year Plan for rapid economic expansion. The CPY expropriated huge amounts of private property. Any factory that worked even a single day during the war years received the label of a "collaborating" business and fell to automatic expropriation by the state. Next, Tito's government seized all property and factories belonging to foreigners, including Yugoslav allies such as the British and Soviets.

The First Five-Year Plan rolled an incredible 27% of Yugoslavia's gross national product back into economic development, 92% of it industrial. This outdid the scope of even the Soviet Union's Five-Year Plans, and caused considerable hardship to large sectors of the populace as production of food and consumer goods dropped to build up a stock of capital goods (manufacturing machinery).

Initially, Tito's slightly unique take on Marxism won praise from the Soviets, as a 1947 article indicated: "The concrete embodiment of the ideas of Marxism regarding the unity of the working class with the majority of working people [...] has been most consistently developed in Yugoslavia where the People's Front unites almost seven million people [...] The People's Front [...] is a social-political organisation of the people in which the working class, headed by the Communist Party, plays a leading role." (Swain, 2011, 90).

However, Yugoslavia soon split with Stalin and the USSR due to Tito's maverick leadership. Tito, in a bid to assist a communist revolution in Greece, effectively invaded Albanian territory to protect Greek communist bases there, without first consulting or even informing either Stalin or Albania's leader Enver Hoxha. Though the Soviets eventually outwardly accepted this action, they began pressuring Tito to add Yugoslavia to a planned Balkan Federation. The Federation, under Soviet control, would effectively reduce all of the member countries, Yugoslavia included, to the helpless provinces of what might be called a "greater Soviet empire." An exchange of letters followed, in which Stalin claimed that the Yugoslavian success in World War II stemmed entirely from the Red Army. In fact, this represented a complete falsehood; the Yugoslavian Partisans largely won the war in their own country independently, while most of what aid they did receive came from the British, not the Soviets, whose support always appeared lukewarm.

The communist Cominform convened in Bucharest on June 28th, 1948 and expelled Yugoslavia from its fold. Though it issued an invitation to Tito and his top lieutenants to attend, Tito refused to travel there, noting "if we have to be killed, we'll be killed on our own soil." (Swain, 2011, 96). That was a clear insight, given Stalin's long history of summoning people to areas he controlled in order to have them killed.

Thus, for several months, Yugoslavia existed in a sort of vacuum, with the Soviet Union looming over it in wrath. Tito already looked towards the Americans, perplexed by the entire affair, to save him from the USSR, declaring, "The Americans are not fools. They won't let the Russians reach the Adriatic." (Banac, 1988, 137). This essentially encapsulated Tito's foreign and domestic policy for the rest of his reign as Yugoslavia's dictatorial president – maintaining a species of communist state while relying on tacit Western support to keep the Soviet juggernaut at bay. Edvard Kardelj, Yugoslavia's Foreign Minister, provided a succinct summary of how his nation could maintain itself as an unaligned state between the two vast power blocs of the 20th century, the free world to the west and the communist world to the east, by leveraging the "tendency among the imperialists to exploit the contradictions between the socialist states, very much in the same way as we wish to exploit the internal contradictions of the imperialist system." (Banac, 1988, 138),

**Kardelj**

The U.S. and England cautiously adopted a "wedge strategy" towards Yugoslavia, supporting it in order to keep it out of the Soviet sphere of influence and put up a roadblock in the way of Stalin's European ambitions. Tito accordingly ceased giving aid to the Greek communist organizations, paid back U.S. Lend-Lease aid, and remunerated English and American people whose property in Yugoslavia had suffered expropriation. Still, the Americans naturally remained cautious of Tito's and Yugoslavia's intentions. They also could not quite decide how to deal with a country that housed a repressive, dictatorial Marxist regime, yet showed strong signs of nationalism and showed itself willing to defy the still-ascendant power of Moscow. As George Frost Kennan, an influential Cold War political strategist, said of Yugoslavia, a "new factor of fundamental and profound significance  has been introduced into the world communist movement by the demonstration that the Kremlin can be successfully defied by one of its own minions (Lees, 1997, 54). By 1955, the US government had given Tito more than $1.2 billion in combined economic and military aid. The English also provided assistance, though on a lesser scale due to their waning power.

Tito's regime gradually moved away from a purely communist approach as the pragmatic demands of survival placed effectiveness ahead of ideology. The Yugoslavians tried a three-year trial period of collective farms, or SRZs, after which they asked the peasants if they wished to stay or leave. Flooded with gigantic numbers of requests to leave, Tito and his cabinet decided to return 1.5 million acres of agricultural land to individual peasant family ownership in 1952. Collective farming vanished in most areas by 1953, with a few notable exceptions.

At around the same time, the Yugoslavian state developed one of its other unique characteristics, the principle of self-management. Under this scheme, many factories worked not at the direction of a cumbersome and dangerous central bureaucracy as in the case of the Soviet Union, but by "workers' councils" elected and staffed by the laborers at the factory themselves.

Showing considerable acuity, Tito declared in 1950 that the USSR actually represented a counterrevolutionary state. Stalin, he said, operated the entire Soviet Union as a gigantic capitalist monopoly. His method, he claimed, placed the means of production into the hands of those Marx intended: the workers themselves. When the West invented the term "Titoism" to describe Tito's rule in Yugoslavia, by contrast, Tito claimed that he represented the true Marxist and that Stalin was the "heretic:" "It is simply that we have added nothing to Marxist-Leninist doctrine. [...] Should 'Titoism' become an ideological line, we would become revisionist; we would have renounced Marxism. We are Marxists, I am a Marxist and therefore I cannot be a 'Titoist.' Stalin is the revisionist: it is he who has wandered from the Marxist road. 'Titoism' as a doctrine does not exist." (Dedijer, 1953, 432).

This, of course, represented something of a semantic dodge, unlike Tito's insightful remark that Soviet communism resembled a gigantic monopolistic corporation. Yugoslavia under Tito matched no other state on the planet. Soon, the workers' councils at the factories received permission to make investments and other business decisions, using the funds their efforts earned, independent of state interference, provided that "ownership" remained divided equally between everyone who worked at the factory and decisions occurred by vote rather than "board of directors" fiat.

On the personal scale, Tito's success with women continued. The Yugoslavian leader met a nurse, Jovanka Budisavljevic, after a gall bladder operation and married her in 1951. Jovanka remained married to Tito for the next 29 years until he died, though their relationship broke down to some degree several years before his death. Jovanka lived until 2013, witnessing both the entirety of Tito's reign and the significant events of the post-Tito era.

**Dragan Zebeljan's picture of Jovanka**

Stalin's death in 1953 while Tito was visiting Britain represented a major change in Soviet leadership. Tito attempted rapprochement with the Soviet Union, only to be largely rebuffed by new Soviet leader Nikita Khrushchev. However, in 1955, Khrushchev visited Belgrade, and, after reaching something of an understanding with Tito, both men signed the Belgrade Declaration. This promulgated an agreement of mutual non-interference, and Khrushchev canceled all of Yugoslavia's debts upon his return to the Soviet Union.

**Khrushchev**

Tito felt safe enough to visit Moscow in 1956, and Khrushchev and Tito continued their diplomatic dance for the rest of the decade, but Yugoslavia – in the person of its leader – steadfastly refused any agreement that would reduce the country's independence. Tito continued playing the East and West off against each other in order to keep his own country essentially safe from major external interference throughout the 1950s.

Tito continued to enjoy the high life as he aged, living in superbly furnished castles, supplying himself with every luxury, and continuing to pursue women besides his wife Jovanka. However, he also continued to pay attention to running his unusual state and addressing problems as they arose. In the early 1960s, the self-management program ran into problems due to the difficulties of allotting investment funds. Officials managed to take over the distribution of these funds, compromising the independence of many self-managed factories. This led to the production of unnecessary or substandard goods as the officials pursued their own agendas without reference to market demand.

**Tito in 1961**

At the same time, consumer demand burgeoned as the economy recovered and the self-management program produced genuinely effective economic activity. Tito waffled for some time, apparently trying to coordinate his efforts with Khrushchev, but the latter's fall removed the likelihood of any cooperation between the Yugoslavian and Soviet economies that would not leave Moscow with the whip hand and strip Tito of his independence.

At the Eighth Party Congress in 1965, Tito increased the amount of money that self-managed factories could retain for investment to 70%, up from the current 30%, thus improving the economic position of the workers and attempting to reduce the power of the officials to interfere in the economy's functioning. The bureaucracy naturally resisted this, wishing to retain its control over investment and thus economic planning and activity.

## Ceaușescu Takes Power

The mid-1950s were tumultuous for the Soviet Bloc. Several countries saw Stalin's death and the apparent change of direction, even the softening of policy under Khrushchev, as an opportunity to pursue a reformist path. In East Germany, Poland, and Hungary, demonstrations against the communist regimes induced uncertainty. In fact, Hungarian leaders attempted to incorporate the protestors and orientate themselves towards the West, leading to a notorious Soviet invasion. The year before, in 1955, Moscow had brought together all the satellites as part of the Warsaw Pact, a collective security organisation to challenge the North Atlantic Treaty Organization (NATO), which had been founded in 1949 by the United States and Western European allies. Romania stayed out of the internal disputes and dutifully signed up to the Warsaw Pact.

Communists did not rise to the top of their parties by stepping outside the policy positions or paradigms of the day. As was shown time and time again, those who took power in the Communist Bloc, particularly in Central Europe and Eastern Europe, proved masters in party management and bureaucratic politics. This was certainly true of Ceaușescu, who charted an unspectacular path in the decade before he took power. He managed to take the prevailing position on major decisions and alienate as few of his colleagues as possible. He was certainly aided by his allegiance to, and support from, General Secretary Gheorghe Gheorghiu-Dej. It was said that Ceaușescu was fawning to his superiors, like Gheorghiu-Dej, and cruel and callous towards his subordinates.

After Khrushchev's agricultural plan, Romania sought to diversify its trading relations in the late 1950s. From a very low base, Romania increased its export trade with the West to 25% of its total by 1958, and that increased to 33% by 1964. Similarly, exports from the West increased to 40% of the total by 1964, which actually exceeded the amount from the Soviet Union itself.[14] Therefore, Romanian communism had a national dimension, in addition to being ideologically Stalinist. In fact, Gheorghiu-Dej fostered cordial relations with American leaders, including President Kennedy and President Johnson, and in this respect, Romania had a similar status in the Cold War as Tito's Yugoslavia, remaining a relatively Western-friendly communist country. This brought Bucharest into confrontation with Moscow, but never severely enough to cause the kind of ruptures seen in other Eastern Bloc states.

This approach made plenty of sense. For comparatively poor countries like Romania and

---

[14] William E. Crowther, *The political economy of Romanian socialism* (Praeger, 1988) p. 61.

Yugoslavia, building relations with West made sense in terms of their own development and sovereignty. There was another dimension to Romania's increasingly ambiguous position under Gheorghiu-Dej, and that was the split between China and the Soviet Union. The basis of the dispute between the communist world's two largest powers, like many other issues, can be traced to Stalin's death and succession. Mao Zedong was very much the junior partner in the relationship after his communists triumphed in the Chinese Civil War in 1949, but Mao took umbrage with Khrushchev's approach towards the capitalist world after he assumed ultimate control of the Soviet party in 1956. Mao, along with other like-minded radicals, accused the Soviets and their allies of "revisionism," and a split developed towards the end of the decade. Tensions increased between the two in the 1960s, and there was even fighting along the huge border the two nations shared.

In addition to being volatile, the split presented opportunities for countries of various stripes to exploit. While the West could seek to drive a wedge in a way that would weaken the Soviets, the Romanians could expand their trading network beyond their post-1945 Soviet dependency, and essentially hedge bets against a number of challenges. By remaining on good terms with China and the USSR, as well as fostering links with Western Europe and the United States, Romania could increase its wealth and develop its economy to a greater extent.

On March 19, 1965, Gheorghe Gheorghiu-Dej died from lung cancer, and inevitably, a struggle for power began behind closed doors. Deputy Prime Minister Gheorghe Apostol believed he was Gheorghiu-Dej's chosen successor, while Prime Minister Ion Gheorghe Maurer also eyed power. In the end, the competing factions at the top of the party settled on a compromise candidate in Nicolae Ceaușescu, who was just 47 and thus the youngest leader in the communist world.[15]

Ceaușescu was very much a General Secretary in the mold of his mentor, Gheorghiu-Dej. His predecessor, however, had relaxed his iron grip over Romanian society in the mid-1960s, during which censorship had been loosened and thousands of political prisoners released. Ceaușescu took power, therefore, as the mood in the country tentatively started to lift, and even with the loosening of restrictions, a significant amount of power rested with the head of the intelligence and internal security services, Alexandru Drăghici.

---

[15] Misha Glenny, *The Balkans 1804-2012: Nationalism, War and the Great Powers* (London: Granta, 2012), p. 598.

**Apostol**

# Drăghici

In the first phase of his time in office, Ceaușescu set about consolidating his power and diminishing the standing of his rivals, particularly those from the older generation. The process took him about three years and required making overtures to more liberal Romanian opinion, as well as nurturing nationalist sentiment. He gradually installed his supporters in positions of influence. Most notably, Ceaușescu denounced Stalinists and their crimes in the country, as a result managing to move Drăghici from the Ministry of Internal Affairs.

The largest reorganization came at the December 1967 party conference, when Ceaușescu increased the number of posts within the state bureaucracy but simultaneously made them more accountable to him. The seeds were therefore sown for an increase in his own personal power. At the same time, Ceaușescu made it easier for Romanians to travel abroad and even introduced an element of private ownership into the economy.[16] The result was a general relaxation of communism in Romania during Ceaușescu's early years. In 1968, Romania was arguably the most liberal country amongst the Warsaw Pact states, perhaps with the exception of Czechoslovakia.

In 1968, reformers took power in Czechoslovakia and started to liberalize a number of features of political and cultural life. Led by Slovak communist Alexander Dubček, the country ushered in an unprecedented degree of openness and dialogue. Dubček called his reforms "socialism with a human face," while the period became commonly known as the "Prague Spring."

Moscow, not surprisingly, perceived the reforms as an existential threat to its influence in the Soviet Bloc, and on August 21, 1968, the Soviets sent forces into Czechoslovakia to reassert control over the country. The Czechoslovakians desperately called for assistance from other communist countries, and even sought aid from the West. They received support from an unlikely source: Nicolae Ceaușescu. The Romanian leader made a speech in Bucharest's Palace Square denouncing the invasion as a "grave danger to peace in Europe, to the fate of socialism in the world."[17] He also called for the formation of a Romanian patriot people's army. Ceaușescu reinforced his message over several days around the country, expressing his support for the Czechoslovak communists and emphasizing his nationalist call to arms, or at least defense.

This most unlikely of leaders managed to stir the Romanian people, and thousands volunteered to fight if their country was the next to be invaded. Romania was seen as a potential target, along with Yugoslavia, because it was viewed as relatively liberal in comparison with other communist states in the region, such as East Germany.[18]

---

[16] Ibid, p. 599.

[17] Misha Glenny, *The Balkans 1804-2012: Nationalism, War and the Great Powers* (London: Granta, 2012), p. 594.

[18] Jussi M. Hanhimaki, *The Rise and Fall of Détente. American Foreign Policy and the Transformation of the Cold War* (Washington DC: Potomac Books), p. 31.

Nevertheless, it was clear Ceaușescu was playing a dangerous game; his public support for Prague enraged the Soviets, who could well have engineered a coup or even a separate invasion. Moreover, the United States and its European allies were never likely to offer Romania any material assistance.[19] Despite the Cold War tension since 1946, and the clear propaganda victory any communist defection would have provided, there had been a general agreement regarding the spheres of influence between Moscow and Washington in Europe. Any incursion into the other side's sphere would have been viewed as a hostile act, and at the time, the Johnson administration was heavily embroiled in the Vietnam War in 1968. Thus, the Americans were anxious to reduce tension with the Soviets, not make things worse by supporting (other than rhetorically) Czechoslovakia, Romania, and Yugoslavia.

As events transpired, the crisis petered out and no further military action took place in Europe. The Soviets had made their point, much to the chagrin of potential reformers in the region. However, Ceaușescu's reputation was enhanced by the fallout, and he had successfully burnished his credentials as a Romanian patriot, increasing his popularity throughout the country. At the same time, in August 1968, Ceaușescu issued a statement setting out his support and friendship with the Soviet Union, thereby pacifying Moscow. Ceaușescu's gamble had apparently paid off, and he would use the political space to strengthen his grip over Romania.

**Ceaușescu's Cult of Personality**

"Up to 1971, by Marxist standards, he was able to generate new ideas within the limits of the system. After his visit to China and North Korea in 1971, something of crucial importance must have happened in his mind. What he saw in North Korea was an image of real socialism- that is, total regimentation. Of course, everything was fundamentally wrong from the beginning. But the practical approaches until 1971 were mitigated by a degree of realism and independent thinking which had not yet become militant and destructive nationalism. I think that all his life he believed in what he considered to be the generous idea of socialism and Communism. But in 1971 he apparently discovered the uses of pyramidal organisation inherent in one-party rule. And he discovered the crucial importance of the top of the pyramid. He hated and despised Stalin who had enjoyed just such a position, but Ceausescu hated Stalin because he saw him as the leader of an Evil Empire. The evilness of it was its imperial character, not its ideology. Hence Ceausescu was blind to his own messianic bent." - Sergiu Celac (Ceausescu's translator), as quoted in John Sweeney's *The Life and Evil Times of Nicolae Ceausescu*

Having staked out his claim for ultimate power within Romanian communism after Gheorghiu-Dej's death in 1965, Ceaușescu was in a strong domestic position by 1970, and his rule would take on its peculiar, idiosyncratic themes over the next decade.

---

[19] Geraint Hughes, *Harold Wilson's Cold War. The Labour Government and East-West Politics, 1964-1970* (Woodbridge: Boydell and Boydell, 2009), p. 149.

In fact, some were even in place by then. Ceaușescu had a hard-line stance towards birth control and abortion, effectively banning it in 1967, proof that despite burnishing liberalizing credentials in the political sphere during the 1960s, Ceaușescu demonstrated a socially conservative attitude towards family matters. Romanian leaders were concerned that the country had a low fertility rate, and this was one attempt to increase the number of children. The impact, however, was that many babies were abandoned, and it led to a notorious institution later known across the world as the Romanian orphanage. It would be one of the longest-lasting and troubling facets of Ceaușescu's legacy. After his regime's fall, there was an estimated minimum of 100,000 children in Romania's orphanages.[20]

Instead of increasing the Romanian workforce, Ceaușescu's policy had a number of deleterious effects. These included the highest maternal mortality rates in Europe, the highest number of deaths from abortion outside the purview of the authorities, and a generation of traumatized children separated from their parents.[21] The abortion law was one of Ceaușescu's most notorious policies, and it had no shortage of competition when it came to his oppressive and cruel policies.

In the early 1970s, Romania had stabilized its foreign relations with the Soviet Union and Warsaw Pact. Nevertheless, Ceaușescu wished to diversify his country's interests and relationships. In some respects, he wanted to follow a similar path to Tito's Yugoslavia,[22] and he was keen on joining the "Non-Aligned Movement," set up in 1961 and dominated by Tito and countries from the developing world who wanted to avoid being drawn into either of the superpowers' spheres of influence.[23] Ceaușescu was never quite able to make the jump, however, knowing that it would likely inflame his sensitive links with Moscow.

Thanks to straddling the line, Ceaușescu had a generally positive reputation abroad. French President General Charles de Gaulle visited Bucharest in 1969 to award Ceaușescu the French "Legion of Honour," while President Nixon also visited the same year.[24]

[20] Wendell Steavenson, 'Ceaușescu's children', *The Guardian*, 10 December 2014, https://www.theguardian.com/news/2014/dec/10/-sp-Ceaușescus-children, [accessed 12 November 2018]

[21] Sharon Maxwell Magnus, 'Ceaușescu's orphans: what a regressive abortion law does to a country', *The Conversation*, 1 February 2017, https://theconversation.com/ceau-escus-orphans-what-a-regressive-abortion-law-does-to-a-country-71949, [accessed 12 November 2018]

[22] R.J. Crampton, *The Balkans since the Second World War*, (Routledge, 2014), p. 138.

[23] David A. Andelman, 'Ceaușescu, Tito Tread Wary and Parallel Paths', 16 April 1978, *New York Times* https://www.nytimes.com/1978/04/16/archives/Ceaușescu-tito-tread-wary-and-parallel-paths.html, [accessed 12 November 2018]

[24] Raluca Besliu, 'Communist Nostalgia in Romania', *Open Democracy*, 13 April 2014, https://www.opendemocracy.net/can-europe-make-it/raluca-besliu/communist-nostalgia-in-romania, [accessed 12 November 2018]

**A 1975 picture of Ceaușescu with French prime minister Jacques Chirac**

Likewise, Ceaușescu was influenced by his sojourns abroad. In 1971 Ceaușescu visited North Korea, North Vietnam, and China, where the three communist countries appeared to exercise total control over their populations with an ideological ferocity unmatched in the European communist world.[25] All three countries were dominated by cults of personality, which gave their leaders enormous personal power.

Each state's particular brand of socialist ideology was closely intertwined and elevated to the level of that central individual. In North Vietnam, Ho Chi Minh, its communist founder, had recently died, but his country would utilise his memory in an ongoing personality cult. North Korea and China, however, took the principle to new heights. In Pyongyang, Ceaușescu saw firsthand the huge crowds that were orchestrated at the behest of leader Kim Il-sung, and the endless posters promoting his image, achievements, and thoughts. China, too, was in the grip of a hyper-personality cult surrounding Chairman Mao Zedong. Mao had precariously initiated the "Cultural Revolution" in the 1960s, which involved groups of radicals denouncing and committing violence against "revisionists" and "capitalist roaders." Waving and reciting Mao's "Little Red Book" of writings, these "Red Guards" were in complete awe of the cult of personality.

---

[25] Misha Glenny, *The Balkans 1804-2012: Nationalism, War and the Great Powers* (London: Granta, 2012), p. 600.

**A picture of Kim Il-sung and Ceaușescu in 1971**

All three countries greatly impressed Ceaușescu in 1971, who has been described as falling into a "political madness" thereafter.[26] When he returned to Romania, Ceaușescu began to develop his own cult of personality, mimicking some of the things he had seen in Asia. He organized mass rallies to reinforce his ultimate power. The country was covered in his image while Ceaușescu, in keeping with the other leaders, started to style himself as a theoretician of Marxist-Leninism.[27] Harking back to 1930s-era Stalinism, Ceaușescu attempted to rewrite history by claiming he and his wife protested against fascism, and photos were even doctored to place Ceaușescu at certain demonstrations. This approach would almost have been comical had it not led to so much misery in his country.

Fresh from his trip, Ceaușescu gave a speech on July 6, 1971 to the Central Committee of the Romanian Communist Party which became known as the "July Theses." Ceaușescu laid out his 17 "Theses" to the party, calling for greater ideological clarity and discipline (almost a Romanian Cultural Revolution), and calling for greater youth communist activity. Ceaușescu

[26] Misha Glenny, *The Balkans 1804-2012: Nationalism, War and the Great Powers* (London: Granta, 2012), p. 601.
[27] Ronald D. Bachman (ed.), Romania: A Country Study. "The Ceaușescu Era" (Washington: Library of Congress, 1989).

denounced the liberalizing reforms of the mid-1960s, favoring more censorship and positioning himself as a Romanian socialist thinker. The July Theses were intended to help him consolidate his grip on power by introducing a number of the principles he had seen in Asia. Ceauşescu would soon have fewer checks on his power, and in tandem with that, his rule would become more erratic. His speech was published in November 1971, and media outlets were quick to follow the party line, declaring a "Golden Era" under Ceauşescu and helping to usher in one of the most unique cults of personality in East Europe or Central Europe during the Cold War. Writers and intellectuals produced works that fawned over Ceauşescu, and events such as the leader's birthday became focal points in the country's calendar.

As Ceauşescu increased his power during the 1970s, his family came steadily more into the public eye. He was unusual within the communist world in that his wife was a prominent figure who wielded real power, and moreover, he aimed to bequeath his office to his son. In July 1971, a key period in the development of Ceauşescu's rule in the country, his wife Elena was elected to the Communist Party's Central Committee, and she continued her rise during the rest of the decade until she became Deputy Prime Minister in 1980. It is said that Mrs. Ceauşescu was more obsessed with publicity and the cult of personality than her husband.

Meanwhile, their heir apparent Nicu, born in 1951, was allegedly a violent, drunken youth, even at school. Of course, the police turned a blind eye to violent crimes he committed with apparent impunity,[28] and Nicu Ceauşescu was being lined up to be Romania's Foreign Minister before beocoming future leader. He too was "elected" to the Party's Central Committee in 1982.

In time, all of them drifted away somewhat from reality, and Nicolae would become suspicious and paranoid, afraid of assassination or a coup. He also became a hypochondriac, terrified of germs and the cold. As a result, Ceauşescu withdrew from contact with others, even colleagues, making it all the more difficult for him to gauge what ordinary Romanians thought of him. It proved to be one of his crucial errors in later years.

---

[28] Ion Mihai Pacepa *Red Horizons: The True Story of Nicolae and Elena Ceauşescu's' Crimes, Lifestyle, and Corruption,* (Regnery, 1990).

**Nicolae and Elena Ceaușescu in Tokyo in 1975 with Emperor Hirohito**

## The couple at a rally

### Ceaușescu's Romania

"It's expensive to keep Communism alive today. I've already got a huge foreign debt staring me in the face, and I can't reduce it by exporting tomatoes or toilet paper. We should be making dollars any way we can. And we should be exporting arms any way and every way, openly and secretly, legally or by smuggling-I don't care how." - Ceaușescu

The first years of Ceaușescu's rule were relatively successful, especially when his entire time in power is considered. The Romanian leader loosened the Party's tight grip over society with liberalizing reforms, and the people were comparatively freer than under the previous regime. Ceaușescu had roused his people's patriotic sentiments with his stand against the invasion of Czechoslovakia in August 1968, and he had successfully avoided direct confrontation with Moscow. He had improved diplomatic ties with a number of countries, including in the West and non-aligned world, and the Romanian economy had expanded and diversified external trade while the country had avoided the worst of the 1973 oil crisis.

Nonetheless, Ceaușescu had already shown himself to be deeply cruel and autocratic in his approach towards social issues, particularly his abortion ban at home, and his trips to see the closed, communist societies of North Vietnam, North Korea and China had fueled a sense of megalomania which would only increase in the 1970s and 1980s. Repression, such as by the security services, or *Securitate*, increased in this period. The best years of Ceaușescu's reign, so far as they can be considered in that way, were over by 1971.

For many countries, 1973 proved a critical year due to OPEC's oil embargo and oil price hike. Romania, on the other hand, was mainly insulated from these problems, as the country had access to its own oil fields and therefore did not feel the price rises as starkly. Although not one of the world's bigger oil producers, Romania did export some of its supplies.

It was here that Romania felt the effects of the crisis as many of its main clients – Western countries – tightened their belts due to stagflation (a stagnating economy, low growth and high inflation) and therefore bought less of its oil.[29] The crisis itself was a result of the 1973 Yom Kippur War between Israel and an alliance of Arab states, which retaliated against the West for its support of Israel with the oil price rises.

The Yom Kippur War was just one piece of what was (and still is) an intractable conflict between Israel and its neighbors in the Middle East, but for Nicolae Ceaușescu in the 1970s, the conflict offered him an opportunity to burnish his credentials as a diplomat and peacemaker.

---

[29] Cornel Ban, 'What brought Romania into Default in 1981?' *European Economics,* 19 May 2012, https://europeaneconomics.wordpress.com/2012/05/19/what-brought-romania-into-default-in-1981/, [accessed 12 November 2018]

Romania had taken a somewhat indifferent stance towards the Arab-Israeli conflict, and in 1967, during the Six Day War, Ceaușescu remained neutral. This was unusual because the two majority groups in the Cold War fell in behind either Israel (the West) or the Arab states (the communist world). Ceaușescu then styled himself as a peace negotiator and met a number of the key protagonists after the 1967 war.

In addition to bolstering his image as an independent leader like Tito, this stance may also have been a vehicle to garner support for his regime in Washington and various European capitals. Although there is evidence that Ceaușescu encouraged the various sides to enter into dialogue, there was criticism that this was the extent of his skills as a diplomat.[30] After the 1973 war, a new phase opened up, one primarily focused on finding a negotiated settlement between Israel and the Arab states, as well as with the Palestinians. American Secretary of State Henry Kissinger had made his name negotiating the end of the Vietnam War, and he now turned his attentions to the Middle East. Kissinger found Ceaușescu a useful figure in his efforts, and Romania offered its territory as a possible venue for talks between Kissinger and the Palestinian leader Yasser Arafat.[31] The meeting never happened, but it demonstrates the ostensibly constructive role Ceaușescu was attempting to play in the region and in world affairs.

In many respects, Ceaușescu's foreign policy followed in the footsteps of Gheorghiu-Dej. Both Romanian leaders viewed a "non-conformist" foreign policy as a means of maintaining stability within the international sphere.[32] In fact, as has already been shown, this principle can be dated back to Romanian authorities shifting allegiances before and during World War I and World War II. Between 1965 and 1985, the number of countries with which Romania had diplomatic relations increased from 67 to 138, while economic relations stretched to 155 states. That said, this trend was accompanied by the highly personal nature of Ceaușescu's rule, particularly after 1971. His foreign policy "achievements," role as a peacemaker and the extent to which he was welcomed to palaces and parliaments around the world enhanced his domestic position and was considered integral to his country's development and prestige.

Although in hindsight the 1970s can be viewed as the period when Ceaușescu turned Romania into an archetypal dictatorship, he was often welcomed by foreign leaders, even feted. The apogee of Ceaușescu's positive reputation on the international stage came with his relationship with the British during the decade. It may be that the British thought that by befriending the Romanian leader they could peel away the country from Moscow's sphere of influence in the Cold War; indeed, the British government had attempted something similar with Tito's

---

[30] Sielke Kelner, 'Ceaușescu and the Six-Day War: The View from Washington and London', *The Wilson Center*, 5 June 2017, https://www.wilsoncenter.org/blog-post/Ceaușescu-and-the-six-day-war-the-view-washington-and-london, [accessed 13 November 2018]

[31] James R. Stocker, 'A Historical Inevitability?: Kissinger and US Contacts with the Palestinians (1973–76)', *The International History Review*, (39:2, 2017, pp. 316-337).

[32] Cezar Stanciu, 'A Rebirth of Diplomacy: The Foreign Policy of Communist Romania between Subordination and Autonomy, 1948–1962', *Diplomacy & Statecraft*, (24:2, 2013, pp. 253-272).

Yugoslavia and later with Poland. A number of treaties and agreements were signed between the two countries in Bucharest and London over the course of the decade that affected economic matters, most notably trade and investment.[33] Britain, in economic trouble during this time, sought to increase its exports to as many places as possible, including communist states like Romania. Ceaușescu was even granted a state visit to the UK in 1978, making him the first communist head of state given this honor. This included a meeting with Queen Elizabeth II, and even, astonishingly, an honorary knighthood. The British government would be left embarrassed (when the full extent of Ceaușescu's oppressive policies became known, and the knighthood was subsequently withdrawn in 1989. A future British Foreign Secretary later said that this episode was the most "dismal disaster in Anglo-Romanian history," and that Ceaușescu had either been mistakenly invited or even invited himself.[34] Regardless, British foreign policy and diplomatic circles were certainly aware of the totalitarian nature of the Romanian regime in the 1970s. Put simply, the British, as well as others, saw a strategic benefit in cultivating close ties with Ceaușescu, no matter how ugly the optics later became.

**Ceaușescu and Queen Elizabeth II**

[33] Mark Percival, 'Britain's "Political Romance" with Romania in the 1970s', *Contemporary European History* (4, no. 1 (1995) pp. 67-87), p. 69.
[34] Geoffrey Howe, *Conflict of Loyalty* (Basingstoke: Macmillan, 1994), p. 428.

Despite holding virtually absolute power in Romania, Ceaușescu had always faced prejudice within the country. Bucharest's elites, particularly the intellectual classes, had looked down upon the barely educated peasant's son from the countryside. Ceaușescu, therefore, may have had some reason to fear an attempted takeover at some point by an establishment resentful of his position.

He had also made himself vulnerable to opprobrium from others in positions of influence in Romania, as well as the public at large. By so closely aligning himself with the government, its policies, and the state, Ceaușescu was opening himself up to direct confrontation and excoriation. Nowhere else in the Communist Bloc could the people directly connect government policies - and its failures – with an individual leader. It was noteworthy, and not altogether surprising, that Ceaușescu would be the only leader to face mob justice as the Soviet Bloc disintegrated at the end of the 1980s.

By the time Ceaușescu actually was deposed, he had already faced several attempts to remove him from power, and the first trouble came due to a high-profile defection and public denunciation in 1978.

At the time, General Ion Mihai Pacepa was a high-ranking member of the Romanian intelligence services as the head of the foreign intelligence unit, a secretary at the Ministry of the Interior, and an advisor to Ceaușescu. In July 1978, Pacepa had been sent by Ceaușescu to relay a message to the German Chancellor Helmut Schmidt, but Pacepa later alleged that he had actually been sent to Bonn to arrange the assassination of the Romanian director of "Radio Free Europe," a Western, Cold War-era propaganda vehicle.

**Pacepa**

Whatever the truth actually was, Pacepa sensationally walked into the U.S. Embassy in Bonn and claimed political asylum. Gleefully accepting communist defectors, the Americans transferred Pacepa to American territory, and when news of the defection reached Ceaușescu, the Romanian leader was said to be apoplectic, even on the verge of a nervous breakdown. Pacepa's action represented a huge blow to the Romanian leader's all-powerful and omnipotent reputation. Ceaușescu ordered the assassination of Pacepa, apparently sending two hit-squads to the United States itself to find the defector, but to no avail.[35] Ceaușescu's Middle Eastern allies, including Arafat and Libyan dictator Muammar Gaddafi, also put ransoms on Pacepa's head, and it has even alleged that the Romanian Securitate brought in the infamous assassin "Carlos the Jackal" to find and kill Pacepa. None of the attempts proved successful, and Pacepa exposed the activities and whereabouts of almost every Romanian spy. By the early 1980s, these foreign intelligence operations were in tatters. In addition, Pacepa gave the fullest picture to date of what life was like in Ceaușescu's Romania. The extent and cruelty of communist repression in the

---

[35] Michael Ledeen, 'Review of Red Horizons Red Horizons, by Ion Mihai Pacepa', *The American Spectator* April 1988, p. 47.

country seriously damaged the status Ceaușescu had spent years cultivating.

Constantin Pîrvulescu damaged Ceaușescu's reputation in a different way. A long-time communist politician who had been the party's General Secretary for a time during the Second World War while Gheorghiu-Dej was in prison, Pîrvulescu made his stand against Ceaușescu at the 1979 "12th Party Congress." Ceaușescu had been made President of Romania in 1974 and sought "reelection" in 1979, which was obviously to be a rubber stamp by a compliant delegation. However, the elderly Pîrvulescu, by this point 84 years old, spoke out at the congress against the reelection of Ceaușescu, complaining that the leader was more interested in his own personal image and interests than the concerns of the Romanian people. This caused an uproar, during which Pîrvulescu was taken from the event and placed under house arrest. Although it appeared that Ceaușescu had managed to quickly deal with the opposition, the Pîrvulescu episode showed how cracks were starting to appear in the façade. Dissatisfaction with Ceaușescu from communist dignitaries in 1979 would prove a harbinger for the much larger dissent that popped up in 1989.

**Pîrvulescu**

When the 1980s began, Ceaușescu clearly thought he had many more years to rule. He had transformed a communist state into something resembling a monarchy, and given that he was still in his early 60s at the start of the decade, Ceaușescu was relatively young compared to his contemporaries. As it turned out, however, the Romanian leader's power was waning.

Ceaușescu had been shocked to his core as a result of the high-profile dissent of the previous two years, which bred a sense of paranoia. At the same time, he delegated more authority to his wife Elena, who appeared to revel in the increased responsibility. Despite the political oppression prevalent in Romania, which had increased during the 1970s, Ceaușescu's Romania had seen some degree of economic growth and better living standards. The country was also endowed with natural resources and agriculture, so many Romanians may have been able to find some material advantages to Ceaușescu's rule.

This image would crumble when the ROmanian economy hit the rocks in the early 1980s. The 1973 oil crisis had not had much impact on the Romanian economy. Bit another oil catastrophe came about after the 1979 Iranian Revolution. Demand had increased in Romania for energy, and the country relied on supplies from the Middle East, first through a cheap deal with the Shah of Iran and then, after the revolution, with Saddam Hussein's Iraq. The Iran-Iraq War, which started in 1980, caused Romania further difficulty.

Aside from energy requirements, Ceaușescu began to borrow heavily on the international markets, making the most of low interest rates. The Romanian leader had used this cheap money and favorable energy deals to rapidly expand his country's industrial base, but it tied the economy to the actions of external actors. Western countries, most notably the United States, decided to tackle their chronic inflationary problems by increasing interest rates to staggering levels, and as Western banks increased their own interest rates in turn, debt repayments became ever harder to service for many governments. At the start of the 1980s, many developing countries struggled to pay the interest on their debt, leading to an era often referred to as the "Debt Crisis."

For its part, Romania had half a billion dollars worth of debt in 1978, and that had risen to $10.4 billion by 1982, equivalent to 28% of its GDP. In 1981, just the interest payments alone accounted for $3 billion. As a result, Romania applied for an IMF loan of some $1.3 billion, only for the IMF board to reneg on it. As Misha Glenny has pointed out, clearly the Western economic institutions had little faith in the reliability of Ceaușescu's regime to honor its commitments.[36]

As a result, the Romanian economy suddenly found itself in deep trouble. By 1982, Ceaușescu was forced to cut spending and redirect foreign currency earnings towards interest repayments.[37] After 1982 Ceaușescu threw most of the Romanian budget into paying down the debt.[38]

---

[36] Misha Glenny, *The Balkans 1804-2012: Nationalism, War and the Great Powers* (London: Granta, 2012), p. 607.
[37] Cornel Ban, 'What brought Romania into Default in 1981?' *European Economics,* 19 May 2012, https://europeaneconomics.wordpress.com/2012/05/19/what-brought-romania-into-default-in-1981/, [accessed 12 November 2018]
[38] Mark Mazower, *The Balkans: From the End of Byzantium to the Present Day* (London: Phoenix, 2001), p. 137.

Consequently, social conditions worsened, including in the country's bleak orphanages.[39]

In times of economic distress in Romania, Ceaușescu's answer was to increase the hours of the workforce without any concomitant wage rise. It was an approach that mirrored Gheorghiu-Dej's infrastructure building of the 1950s, but the quality of living began to show signs of strain in the 1980s. Power cuts became common, and public transportation was dramatically overcrowded. Bitterly cold winters were endured with drastically reduced heating, and shortages became common. By the winter of 1987, gas consumption in Bucharest was limited to just two hours per day,[40] as fuel was rationed so that the regime could export oil in its desperate efforts to earn foreign currency. If Ceaușescu declared that the temperature was greater than 10 degrees Celsius, burning fuel was prohibited, and those who disobeyed the orders were likely to be prosecuted.[41]

Ceaușescu even planned to reduce the average Romanian's food intake to get through the economic crisis. The "Rational Eating Programme" centrally planned limits on calorie intake, reducing these across 1982-1985 by 9-15%.[42] Supermarkets had empty shelves and little available food, so Romanians began to scavenge for food. All the while, Nicolae and Elena lived in opulent palaces and surroundings, inevitably stirring resentment.

In the same vein, Ceaușescu turned the screws in terms of individual freedom. Romanian society was already deeply repressed, but the Romanian president then decided to ban typewriters, presumably in an attempt to prevent dissenting opinions being published or circulated.[43] Land and property was confiscated and sold, and aesthetically pleasing buildings in Bucharest were destroyed.[44] These were replaced by high rise apartments. Romania was particularly affected by a trend seen across the communist world of brutalist blocks of flats constructed to replace stylish houses and streets.

Naturally, the mood in Romania by the early-mid 1980s was grim. To watch over the embattled Romanian people, Ceaușescu dramatically increased the size of the Securitate, which employed around 24,000 people by the end of his rule and used many more thousands of informants.[45] Surveillance by neighbours, friends, and even family members was commonplace. British Foreign Secretary Geoffrey Howe outlined his view of Ceaușescu's Romania when he visited in 1985 and subsequently called Bucharest the "most inhospitable city I have ever visited." He noted that he had to wear his coat even indoors due to the bitter cold and lack of

---

[39] Wendell Steavenson, 'Ceaușescu's children', *The Guardian*, 10 December 2014, https://www.theguardian.com/news/2014/dec/10/-sp-Ceaușescus-children, [accessed 12 November 2018]

[40] Misha Glenny, *The Balkans 1804-2012: Nationalism, War and the Great Powers* (London: Granta, 2012), p. 607.

[41] Godfrey Hodgson, *People's Century: From the dawn of the century to the eve of the millennium* (Godalming: BBC Books, 1998), p. 597.

[42] Misha Glenny, *The Balkans 1804-2012: Nationalism, War and the Great Powers* (London: Granta, 2012), p. 607.

[43] Godfrey Hodgson, *People's Century: From the dawn of the century to the eve of the millennium* (Godalming: BBC Books, 1998), p. 597.

[44] Ibid, p. 597.

[45] Misha Glenny, *The Balkans 1804-2012: Nationalism, War and the Great Powers* (London: Granta, 2012), p. 604.

heating.[46] Howe's meeting with the "mechanical" Ceauşescu was "deeply depressing."[47]

The rest of the Communist Bloc, including the Soviet Union, experienced something similar during this period. The Cold War seemed to be heating up as President Reagan took a stronger stance against a suspicious, ageing Soviet leadership. One particular catalyst was the Soviet invasion of Afghanistan in December 1979, ostensibly to buttress the country's communist government. The incursion led to howls of protest in the West, as well as a renewed commitment to confront the Soviets and its allies. Moreover, both sides were engaged in an arms race, which also featured hostile military exercises and aggressive rhetoric and propaganda.

Perversely for Ceauşescu, the Cold War gave his country a geopolitical importance as part of the Warsaw Pact and with a regional influence as a "non-conformist." Romania's status as a country that dealt with both sides took on more importance in the early 1980s. The newest kinds of nuclear missiles were deployed in Europe by both sides, leading to the kind of potential standoff that posed problems for countries caught in the middle.

Leadership was crucial in the final phase of the Cold War. The Soviet Union, in keeping with the communist bloc in general, churned out turgid, unimaginative, gerontocrats. Leonid Brezhnev had died in office in 1982 as Soviet general secretary, as did both of his successors, Yuri Andropov in 1984 and Konstantin Chernenko the following year. Chernenko, in particular, appeared to be frail even upon taking office. At the same time, in the United States, Reagan came to power promising to revitalize his own country and stand up to the communist world. As a result, a new arms race began, pitting Reagan against paranoid Soviet leaders who were, no doubt, disturbed by American pronouncements that their sphere was an "Evil Empire". In this final escalation of the Cold War, Germany once more became a focal point when the Soviets deployed a new nuclear weapon–intermediate ballistic SS-20 missiles–into the territory of their Warsaw Pact allies. NATO, after much deliberation and numerous protests, responded in kind by deploying Pershing missiles into West Germany.

Tensions rose elsewhere in Europe also, beginning with a worker's revolt in Poland that demanded separate trade union recognition, dubbed *Solidarity*. As demonstrations continued throughout 1980-81, the Polish communist government ultimately declared martial law, partly because it feared another Soviet intervention like the one in Czechoslovakia in 1968.

It was not obvious to the outside world that the Soviet Bloc was teetering in the 1980s. Clearly, the Soviet Union and its clients still represented a significant military threat, hence the missile deployment, and Ronald Reagan and Margaret Thatcher continued taking a tough tone. Reagan famously called the USSR the "Evil Empire." This heated rhetoric, however, was turned down a notch when Mikhail Gorbachev became General Secretary of the Soviet Union in 1985.

---

[46] Geoffrey Howe, *Conflict of Loyalty* (Basingstoke: Macmillan, 1994), p. 428.
[47] Ibid, p. 428.

**Gorbachev**

Gorbachev reflected a new type of leader in the Soviet Union, in some ways reflecting the "Helsinki Effect," and the impact of the human rights discourse in the 1970s. Gorbachev launched a number of liberalizing policies, such as Glasnost ("openness"), Perestroika ("restructuring") and Uskoreniye ("acceleration"), and they ushered in a new atmosphere in the USSR.[48]

Obviously, Gorbachev looked for new ways to run both the economy and society in the Soviet Bloc. He was acutely aware of the effects high military spending had on the economy, and he was worried Reagan's Strategic Defense Initiative ("Star Wars") would neutralize the Soviet's arsenal.[49] These concerns lcd to a number of policy changes, as well as domestic liberalization, and Gorbachev met with Reagan, Thatcher, and eventually President George H.W. Bush to find ways to secure nuclear disarmament and end the arms race. He made a speech to the United Nations in 1988 in which he promised to withdraw Soviet troops from East Europe,[50] and he

[48] Godfrey Hodgson, *The People's Century: From the dawn of the century to the eve of the millennium* (Godalming: BBC Books, 1998), p. 588.
[49] Ibid, p. 589.
[50] The Gorbachev Visit; Excerpts From Speech to U.N. on Major Soviet Military Cuts, 8 December 1988, [accessed 26 October 2017], http://www.nytimes.com/1988/12/08/world/the-gorbachev-visit-excerpts-from-speech-to-un-

declared the USSR would no longer interfere in Warsaw Pact countries' affairs.[51]

Gorbachev apparently took a more relaxed approach to Soviet control of its Central European and East European satellites, which became formalized at the end of 1988 when he gave a speech to the United Nations General Assembly on December 7 that would have genuinely revolutionary implications. As well as endorsing the Helsinki process and human rights, the Soviet leader announced he was withdrawing all his forces from Afghanistan. He then turned to Central Europe and Eastern Europe and said, "By agreement with our Warsaw Treaty allies, we have decided to withdraw by 1991 six tank divisions from East Germany, Czechoslovakia and Hungary, and to disband them. Assault landing troops and several other formations and units, including assault crossing units with their weapons and combat equipment, will also be withdrawn from the groups of Soviet forces stationed in those countries."[52]

This essentially marked the end of the "Brezhnev Doctrine" that had been in existence since the invasion of Czechoslovakia in 1968. In effect, Gorbachev had granted these countries autonomy from the USSR, which was later reinforced by another Soviet official in 1989, who had declared the "Sinatra Doctrine." Pursuant to this, the Central European and Eastern European states could, to quote the American crooner Frank Sinatra, "go their own way".[53] This effectively ended the Soviets' hold over Poland, Hungary, Czechoslovakia, East Germany, and Romania, and it also opened these nations' regimes up to challenge from opposition groups.

At that stage, it was unclear as to how people in these countries might respond, but Ceauşescu would be one of the first to find out.

**Yugoslavia in the 1980s**

Tito returned to a measure of centralization in the final decade of his life. Though self-management remained a key portion of the Yugoslavian economy, the 1974 Constitution made the state's structure much more hierarchal, giving Tito the power to resist change and try to keep his creation as an unchanging structure for the rest of his life. The Constitution also named Tito president for life in its first article.

Tito continued to enjoy his extravagant lifestyle during the final decade of his life. However, he no longer had the energy of youth and his infinitely complex system began to ossify without his constant tinkering and guidance. The dissident Milovan Djilas noted, "In the late 1960s, Yugoslavia had another chance, the most promising if also the most uncertain, at democratisation … [but by] the early 1970s Tito more firmly than ever held back the movement for change; he

---

on-major-soviet-military-cuts.html?pagewanted=all
[51] Mary Fulbrook, *History of Germany, 1918-2000: the divided nation* (Oxford: Blackwell, 2002), p. 261.
[52] The Gorbachev Visit; Excerpts From Speech to U.N. on Major Soviet Military Cuts, 8 December 1988, [accessed 26 October 2017], http://www.nytimes.com/1988/12/08/world/the-gorbachev-visit-excerpts-from-speech-to-un-on-major-soviet-military-cuts.html?pagewanted=all
[53] Mary Fulbrook, *History of Germany, 1918-2000: the divided nation* (Oxford: Blackwell, 2002), p. 261.

forced creative social, national and individual potentialities to revert to the withered ideals of his youth." (Swain, 2011, 189). Nevertheless, Yugoslavia enjoyed nearly first-world standards of living and a unique system of "self-management" that did not match either communist or capitalist designs. Regardless of its flaws and Tito's human failings, Josip Broz had created a relatively prosperous state that remained separate from the problems of other Cold War countries east or west.

Tito died in early 1980 at 88 years of age, killed by gangrene caused by a leg amputation following arterial blockage. An enormous number of heads of state, including 31 presidents and four kings, attended the funeral of the Croatian machinist who had witnessed and participated in the most tumultuous events of the 20th century. In the end, however, Marshal Tito's unified, multicultural Yugoslavia scarcely survived his death itself. The removal of his strong, unifying personality and its emblematic value for the state enabled the "ethnonationalism" of various racial and religious groups to reassert itself. In the course of less than a human generation, Tito's Yugoslavia shattered, first through political disintegration, and later to the sound of rifles and machine guns.

Tito's death was certain to create a power vacuum in Yugoslavia. He had attempted to stabilize the country's politics with a new constitution in 1974 that set out a collective, rotating leadership, but he also failed to appoint a political successor. The settlement worked for a few years, but several shocks, political and economic, caused fault lines to appear, and these issues worsened as politicians started to agitate nationalist bases in the 1980s. The end of the Cold War further weakened Yugoslavia, leading the country to the brink of disaster.

In fact, as soon as Tito died in 1980, nationalist émigré groups were hailing, predicting or calling for the demise of Yugoslavia.[54] Several countries were home to significant expatriate groups, particularly the Croat organizations. The first actual post-Tito unrest, however, took place in Kosovo in 1981. Ethnic Albanian groups, particularly students, protested against a range of issues, including history teaching and using the Albanian language. The subsequent riots disturbed the elites in Belgrade, as well as the minority Serbs in Kosovo.[55] The province's place in Serb history gave it particular significance as the birthplace of a conscious Serb nation, following their battle with the invading Ottomans in 1389. That Serbs may be losing their privileged position in the province, or even being threatened or persecuted by ethnic Albanians, led to acute sensitivity. A trend missing during the years of the socialist Federation was Serb nationalism. When it returned, the edifices holding Yugoslavia together began to crumble.

It was something altogether less emotive that first debilitated Yugoslavia in the post-Tito years: the economy. It may appear as if the state only faltered after Tito's death, but the 1980s were in

---

[54] John R. Lampe, *Yugoslavia as History: Twice there was a country* (Cambridge: Cambridge University Press, 2000), p. 299.

[55] Carole Rogel, *The Breakup of Yugoslavia and its Aftermath* (London: Greenwood Press, 2004), p. 17.

fact the fruition of many of the dictator's policies. Tito had allowed Yugoslavia to live beyond its means for years and acquired a liking for foreign debt. He was somewhat different from his peers because he effectively shared income with his people. However, when Western banks had to contend with high interest rates in the late 1970s and early 1980s, pressure was inevitably passed on to debtors, including Yugoslavia. By 1983, the country was in serious economic trouble.

The impact of Yugoslavia's economic frailty was not immediately obvious. The country successfully hosted the 1984 Winter Olympic Games in Sarajevo, glorifying in its mantra of brotherhood and multinational and multi-religious harmony.[56] By this time, however, the Federation lacked any substantial figures. In many ways, in the mid-1980s, it resembled other Central European and Eastern European countries, as party functionaries in bland suits talked about unlikely production targets and factory output. This political impotence and latent economic problems – high inflation, low productivity, high debt and need for hard currency – would culminate in the horrors of the 1990s' conflicts when exploited by nationalists. Initially, however, the nationalist impulse was one of self-preservation by weak communist politicians. The most notable – or infamous - example of a career communist who turned to nationalism during the decade was Slobodan Milošević.

**Milošević**

---

[56] Zlatko Jovanovic, 'The 1984 Sarajevo Winter Olympics and Identity-Formation in Late Socialist Sarajevo', *The International Journal of the History of Sport* (34:9, 2017, pp. 767-782).

Slobodan Milošević was born in 1941 in Serbia, then occupied by the Nazis during the Second World War. He became active in the Yugoslav Communist Party youth section during the 1960s while he was at university in Belgrade. At this time, he became acquainted with Ivan Stambolić, whose uncle Petar Stambolić was a key member of the Serbian communist executive.

Starting in local politics, Milošević worked his way up to prominence in Serbian politics by the 1980s. Yugoslavia may have been nominally an egalitarian socialist state, but connections were often important in career progression. Milošević had essentially been mentored by Ivan Stambolić and, using his uncle, began to scale the ladder of Yugoslav communism. Interestingly, in light of later events, Stambolić was considered a "liberal" within the spectrum of Yugoslav politics. By the time of his death in 2006, Milošević had made a reputation with his own particularly virulent form of nationalism, far from the communism of fraternity and brotherhood he embraced in his youth.

By 1984, he had been elevated to a leadership position in Belgrade, and in 1986 Milošević was voted President of the Serbian League of Communists. The structures of Yugoslav politics were complex and multi-layered, but essentially each republic had its own parliament and leadership which then appointed a delegate to the rotating central committee. Thus, by 1986, Milošević was in a position of some influence in Serb politics, the biggest of the Yugoslav republics, but as he moved into power, the direction of Serb society was taking a radical shift. Since the 1930s, it had been accepted that Serb nationalism would be lethal to the Yugoslav project, so for 50 years Tito and his successors had worked to satisfy the various republics and nationalities without allowing Serbs to dominate the Federation. This was, of course, difficult since Serbia was the most populous component part of Yugoslavia. This fragile, but successful, bargain lasted until the mid-1980s, when a number of Serb academics attempted to revise, or revisit, the country's history.

In 1986, the notorious SANU (translated as the Serbian Academy of Sciences) memorandum was published. The document, written by a number of academics and thinkers, aired several long-standing, suppressed Serb grievances.[57] It claimed that Edvard Kardelj (identified as a "Slovene") and Tito (a "Slovene" and a "Croat") had colluded in an attempt to keep the Serbs in a position of relative weakness in Yugoslavia. The document cited the position of Kosovo and its decoupling from Serbia in the 1974 constitution, a situation that enraged Serb national sentiment.[58] SANU berated the role of "fascist" Croats, both during the Second World War and afterwards. It revisited the old theme of centralization of power (favored by Serbs) and devolution (preferred by most of the republics). The SANU memorandum included contributions from 1960s-era Praxis intellectuals. Back in the turmoil of the 1960s, writers such as Mihailo Marković were considered reformers, but by the mid-1980s they had morphed into purveyors of virulent Serb

[57] Laura Silber and Allan Little, *The Death of Yugoslavia* (London: Penguin, 1995), p. 31; 'SANU Memorandum', http://central.gutenberg.org/articles/SANU_Memorandum, (accessed 7 January 2016)
[58] Carole Rogel, *The Breakup of Yugoslavia and its Aftermath* (London: Greenwood Press, 2004), pp. 16-17.

nationalism, while Yugoslav communists, including Serbs like Ivan Stambolić, condemned the document.

It was into this background that Milošević stepped. As Serbian Communist Party chief from 1986, he certainly would have felt pressure at home to take a more assertive approach in his dealings with the other republics. He also may have seen the opportunity to garner and solidify support within Serbia by asserting nationalist claims. It was exactly this dynamic that other Yugoslav leaders had attempted to curtail as far back as the 1930s. Slobodan Milošević would eventually go down the path towards national chauvinism. The first real opportunity he had to state his nationalist credentials was over Kosovo. The Serb nation had eulogized the role the "Field of Blackbirds" had played in defining who the Serbs were, and this battlefield, in Kosovo, had been the place where Serbs had resisted Ottoman marauders all the way back in 1389. Therefore, Serb nationalists were unhappy when Tito separated Kosovo from the Serbian Yugoslav republic in his 1974 constitution.

Ironically, the document was an attempt to decentralise power in Yugoslavia and dilute the kind of nationalist agitation seen during the Croatian Spring, which lasted from 1968-1971. By the 1980s, Kosovo was inhabited by a majority (90%) of ethnic Albanians and a minority (approximately 10%) of Serbs. The former had demonstrated in 1981, demanding greater recognition of the Albanian language and historical tradition in education. The authorities had cracked down severely on these demonstrations, but the episode made clear that the Kosovo issues were likely to come up again at a later date.

In 1987, it was the turn of the Serbs in Kosovo to protest. Demonstrating against alleged persecution by ethnic-Albanians, the Serbs demanded action and protection from the (predominantly ethnic Albanian) police force.[59] Their calls were answered by an unlikely source: Milošević himself. The Serb President, Ivan Stambolić, decided to start a dialogue with the protestors and despatched his trusted lieutenant Milošević to Kosovo. Milošević gave an apparently impassioned plea against nationalism in Kosovo, although he initially appeared unwilling to meet with the local Serb protestors.[60] Nevertheless, after complaints from some Serbs, he agreed to meet the nationalists against the orders of Stambolić. Milošević's stance clearly changed as he decided to explicitly back the Serb nationalists, enraging Yugoslav communists across the Federation. Still in Kosovo, at a meeting with the Serbs expressing their grievances, Milošević was informed that police were beating demonstrators on the streets. Going to the scene of the alleged violence, Milošević asserted, "No one shall dare beat you again!" Broadcast across state television that evening, Milošević became, almost by accident, the defender of the Serbs. He would cultivate this image remorselessly over the next 15 years.

---

[59] *The Sydney Morning Herald*, 'The rise and fall of Milošević', 12 March 2006, https://www.smh.com.au/world/the-rise-and-fall-of-Milošević-20060312-gdn4y1.html [accessed 30 October 2018]
[60] Laura Silber and Allan Little, *The Death of Yugoslavia* (London: Penguin, 1996)

**Stambolić**

As Milošević sought to increase his personal power in Belgrade, Stambolić attempted to discipline Milošević, grievously concerned over Yugoslavia's fate if his deputy continued along a nationalist path. A public criticism was delivered to Milošević on state news, but this elicited a fiery response. Milošević accumulated support for his nationalist approach towards Kosovo and began to undermine Stambolić. Dragiša Pavlović, a Stambolić ally, was expelled from the Communist Party over his attitude towards Kosovo. Milošević claimed that Pavlović was soft on Albanian radicals, and Milošević also began to install loyalists into bureaucratic and advisory positions. Stambolić himself was then sacked, nominally because of a letter he had written in support of Pavlović, but in reality as a political power grab by Milošević, who succeeded him as

President of Serbia within the Yugoslav Federation. In 1988-1989, Milošević launched his so-called "anti-bureaucratic revolution" which mostly entailed removing the old guard and putting his allies into power in Vojvodina, Kosovo and Montenegro.[61] In a remarkably short space of time, Milošević had transformed himself from a dull party functionary into a Serb nationalist capable of overturning the ruling elites in the surrounding republics and accruing ever more personal power and influence.

Many books about the fall of Yugoslavia emphasize the role played by the end of the Cold War from 1989-1991, but it is important to recognise that nationalist agitation had already started to surge in Yugoslavia while the status quo in Central Europe and Eastern Europe still existed. The winds of Gorbachev's *Glasnost* – or openness – reforms blew across the communist world during this time, and a desire for greater freedom in many countries led to the overthrow of the authorities in favor of democracy and market capitalism. In Yugoslavia, the desire for greater personal autonomy seamlessly transformed into group demands, essentially national self-determination. This proved intractable since the different peoples of Yugoslavia did not live in discrete territories, and also because several of these prerogatives lent on a maximalist claim of a "Greater Croatia," a "Greater Serbia," and so on. The umbrella of socialism suppressed, for the most part, national competition in the Yugoslav Federation, which had always existed but had simply been dormant.

The growing sense of Serb domination in Yugoslavia, particularly under the aegis of Milošević, concerned the other republics. In February 1989, Slovenian leader Milan Kučan stormed out of a central committee meeting in protest. Kučan's subsequent speech defended the rights of ethnic Albanians in Kosovo, as well as his own people's autonomy, the Slovenes. Deemed inflammatory, this brought Serb protestors out onto the streets of Belgrade. Shortly afterwards, the Kosovo and Vojvodina assemblies were forced to accept constitutional changes that increased Belgrade's influence over their affairs. The short-lived period, after 1974, of greater autonomy for these two republics was over.

---

[61] John B. Allcock, *Explaining Yugoslavia* (London: Hurst & Company, 2000), p. 427.

**Kučan**

Milošević continued to set about consolidating his own prestige amongst the Serbs. On June 28, 1989, marking the 600th anniversary of the Battle of Kosovo, Milošević spoke to a million Serbs at a rally on the Polje battlefield itself.

Serbia was not the only Yugoslav republic to see a rise in nationalism in the 1980s. Almost across the board, nationalist sentiment grew in Yugoslavia in the decade after Tito died. The geopolitical importance of Yugoslavia declined as the West and the Soviets under Gorbachev moved towards a new détente after 1985, and there were the economic factors that eroded Yugoslav's living standards and led to a loss of faith in the federal system. One could point to structural flaws in the whole Yugoslav project, and that the country's history after 1918 had been a series of short term measures to prevent an inevitable dissolution. Nevertheless, putting all these structural factors to one side, individuals, personalities, and human agency were clearly crucial in undermining the legitimacy of socialist Yugoslavia.

First and foremost was the role played by Milošević, but other republics also played their part. In Croatia, the independently-minded group of intellectuals and agitators who rose to prominence in the Croatian Spring had been imprisoned, expelled from influential positions, or sidelined after 1971. This most likely hardened the positions of many Croat nationalists in favor of total separation from Yugoslavia. Backed by a large diaspora, particularly in the Federal

Republic of Germany, émigré groups and a considerable funding apparatus, the support network was already in place for any move towards greater autonomy for Croatia.

This was embodied in the late 1980s by Franjo Tudjman.[62] An academic and Croat cultural nationalist, Tudjman had played a key role in the 1960s' disturbances, only to have been stripped of his military rank and imprisoned on more than one occasion after the Croatian Spring. Tudjman, however, was a hugely controversial figure.[63] In the 1980s, he started to articulate the fixtures and fittings of a Croatian state. These included the flag from the Ustaše era. Having brutally committed ethnic cleansing against the Serbs during its time in power between 1941-1945, invoking the Ustaše was an inflammatory, ill-judged move. Around 12% of Croatia's population, almost 600,000 people, were ethnic Serbs, and it is not difficult to imagine how any invocation of Ustaše or the NDH (referring to the wartime, proto-fascist Independent State of Croatia) regime invoked terror and horrific memories within those communities. In response, Serb nationalist intellectuals branded Croats part of a "genocidal nation."[64]

**Franjo Tudjman**

Slovenia, under Milan Kučan, also moved towards autonomy in the 1980s. Feeding on sentiment across the communist world, Slovenian media called for greater democratization and respect for human rights after 1987.[65] Kučan also took his controversial stance towards Kosovo,

---

[62] Carole Rogel, *The Breakup of Yugoslavia and its Aftermath* (London: Greenwood Press, 2004), pp. 141-142.

[63] Carole Rogel, *The Breakup of Yugoslavia and its Aftermath* (London: Greenwood Press, 2004), p. 142.

[64] Vesna Drapac, *Constructing Yugoslavia: A Transnational History*, (Basingstoke: Palgrave Macmillan, 2010), p. 250.

[65] Viktor Meier, *Yugoslavia. A History of its Demise*, translated by Sabrina Ramet, (London: Routledge, 1995), p. 59.

which set Slovenia against the Serbs and Milošević. Slovenia was the most economically developed part of Yugoslavia and was confident it could prosper alone. It also did not share a border with Serbia, and it was relatively homogeneous ethnically (meaning it did not contain a big contingent of any other Yugoslav national minority), potentially shielding it from aggression. Once Yugoslavia began to destabilize after 1987, Slovenia saw its opportunity to break away. Kučan presented himself as a civilized democrat and the voice of reason, and clearly Slovenia's path to independence was markedly different than other republics. Thus, in his own way, Kučan played a key part in the breakup of Yugoslavia.[66]

Meanwhile, nationalist leaders had moved towards positions of influence in other parts of the Federation, such as Bosnian Serb leader Radovan Karadžić, who formed the Serb Democratic Party (SDS) in 1989.

Despite the issues, at the end of the 1980s, the fragile peace in Yugoslavia still held. It was in the economic sphere that the country appeared to be fraying.

### Ceaușescu's Demise

"You need not admit your mistakes, mister. In 1947, we assumed power, but under completely different circumstances. In 1947, King Michael showed more dignity than you. And you might perhaps have achieved the understanding of the Romanian people if you had now admitted your guilt." – An excerpt of prosecutor Gica Popa's statement at Ceaușescu's trial

As Gorbachev changed the Soviet Union's direction, the Romanian economy was experiencing grave distress by the mid-1980s. As a result of Ceaușescu's corruption and policies, his people were suffering through shortages and daily ordeals just to survive, yet as the situation became ever more serious, Ceaușescu embarked upon his largest show of opulence by commissioning the Palace of the Parliament. Started in 1984, Ceaușescu ordered the building of an enormous central palace in Bucharest, and when it was finished, it would stand as the world's third largest administrative building. In order to clear space to build his structure, Ceaușescu evicted 40,000 people from their homes and bulldozed 14 churches and a synagogue.[67] The building was not finished until 1997, several years after Ceaușescu's death, and it has since been described as a "monstrosity."[68]

---

[66] John R. Lampe, *Yugoslavia as History. Twice there was a country.* (Cambridge: Cambridge University Press, 2000), pp. 332.

[67] Misha Glenny, *The Balkans 1804-2012: Nationalism, War and the Great Powers* (London: Granta, 2012), p. 608.

[68] Ibid, p. 608.

**The Palace of the Parliament**

This was hardly the only example of Ceaușescu's delusions of grandeur. It was clear by the mid-1980s that he had lost his grip on the realities of his policies. His abortion ban was a long-standing measure that had brought much suffering to many in Romania, and Ceaușescu ordered that women under the age of 45 were expected to have at least five children. This mandate was accompanied by compulsory gynaecological inspections.[69]

Ceaușescu's strategy, such as it was, found itself running out of road. Dissent was rising, despite the regime's best efforts to silence any kind of opposition, and in 1984, the military, led by General Nicolae Militaru, attempted to overthrow Ceaușescu in a planned coup.[70] The military unit sent to oust the Romanian leader, however, was redeployed, so the coup was called off.

In May 1987, Gorbachev visited Romania, and this visit showed the stark contrast between the Stalinist condition of the Romanian Communist Party and the new ideas Gorbachev was trying to promote. During a tense meeting with the Romanian Communist Party, the various officials and high-ranking party members offered formulaic and submissive praise for their leader Ceaușescu. The stage-managed sycophancy annoyed Gorbachev, who criticized and lectured the comrades on the state of the country and the poor-quality goods available.[71] These events were mirrored

---

[69] Godfrey Hodgson, *People's Century: From the dawn of the century to the eve of the millennium* (Godalming: BBC Books, 1998), p. 597.

[70] John Simpson, 'Ten Days that Fooled the World', *The Independent* 16 December 1994, https://www.independent.co.uk/life-style/ten-days-that-fooled-the-world-1387659.html, [accessed 14 November 2018]

across the region, as Gorbachev would visit the countries concerned about the stagnating conditions and advise party leaders to reform. Simultaneously, Gorbachev withdrew the Soviet security guarantee for Warsaw Pact countries. It had been Ceaușescu himself who had denounced the Soviet-led invasion of Czechoslovakia in 1968, but in 1989, it is likely he preferred that kind of arrangement still existed.

To cope with the growing difficulties within Romania, Ceaușescu and his wife Elena utilized more grotesque forms of repression, even as they continued living a luxurious life far removed from the average Romanian. It had been many years since Ceaușescu understood the everyday concerns of his people, and Ceaușescu ruled the country so tyrannically that Romania produced fewer dissidents and anti-regime movements than in neighbouring communist nations, but even this changed in the late 1980s.

Although they could hardly be labeled liberals, or even reformers, an open letter was circulated in March 1989 criticising Ceaușescu. The so-called "Letter of the Six" was organised by Silviu Brucan and five other communist dignitaries, including Constantin Pîrvulescu, who had notoriously denounced the Romanian leader in 1979. The letter outlined a left-wing critique of Ceaușescu, disparaging the regime for its ineffectiveness and lack of socialist humanism. Unsurprisingly, Ceaușescu was outraged by this show of dissent and banished the six to various corners of the country

The letter itself was broadcast on Radio Free Europe and seen as a significant development by outside observers, but there is little evidence the letter had any direct impact on the general population. Ceaușescu apparently managed to see off that crisis, but he could not forestall the inevitable.

Very few observers, commentators, or political scientists saw the end of communism in Europe coming in 1989. This was partly because there was such a scarcity of reliable information from most of these hermetically sealed totalitarian nations, and partly because the end came so quickly. Most of the communist regimes had similaritie, namely: centrally planned economies, repressive internal security agencies, and censorship. There were, however, significant differences. Hungary had made a number of economically liberal reforms by 1988 and had removed its hard border with neighboring Austria in 1989. Poland also responded to the vocal Solidarity trade union movement and moved into a period of détente in 1988-1989, with negotiations and elections in mid-1989. Czechoslovakia had long been a hotbed for anti-totalitarian dissent. East German citizens were long repressed by the all-purveying security apparatus, especially the Stasi, but even they began to flee to West Germany through Hungary in the summer of 1989, as well as holding demonstrations in cities such as Dresden and Leipzig

---

[71] Celestine Bohlen, 'Gorbachev challenged by Romania', *The Washington Post*, 28 May 1987, https://www.washingtonpost.com/archive/politics/1987/05/28/gorbachev-challenged-by-romania/39020705-b8eb-470c-9244-e98f4257ce97/?utm_term=.823b4c8dafb3, [accessed 14 November 2018]

soon afterwards.

The communist system, therefore, had been fragmenting before the end of 1989, but the focal point for its demise was the fall of the Berlin Wall in November 1989. In the years following the fall of the Berlin Wall, many writers have taken the time to analyze the event chronologically. Just how did the messages about the easing of travel restrictions get to the people? What was the East German government's intention versus how was it implemented by the people who carried it out? Before attempting an answer to these questions, it is important to note that the fall of the Berlin Wall was in no way inevitable, at least in the sense of when and how it took place. Timothy Garten Ash cautions his *Guardian* readers regarding the tendency to view it this way, writing that "it is almost impossible to recreate the emotional intensity of the moment of liberation. For that intensity came from having lived for most, if not all, your life with the aching certainty that something like this was, precisely, impossible".[72]

In another warning to readers who assume the fall of the wall was simply a foregone conclusion, historian David Clay Large reminds his readers that East Germany and its leaders had perhaps the least reason to believe they were in danger. Honecker, Large claims, had a great amount of credibility as the head of Germany since the end of World War II, and had done a very effective job at squelching dissidence. As had been the practice of East Germany since the construction of the Berlin Wall and the accompanying economic struggles, dissidents could become prisoners, who would then become saleable goods to West Germany.[73] The severity of response to those who desired escape and the internal intimidation of East Germans in their workplaces, homes, and even churches gave many Germans reason enough to believe that they would live and die in the shadow of the wall. After 28 years, there were now many living who had never known a day without it.

In the end, however, the pressure mounted on even East Germany to make concessions. Though Honecker disagreed with Gorbachev's reform attempts, it was still difficult when "GDR authorities found themselves in the awkward position of trying to curtail contacts between East German citizens and the mother country of Communism".[74] The people of East Germany had limited chances for public gatherings without strict control. In January of 1988, East German leaders had gathered to honor the communist radical Rosa Luxemburg. When a number of protestors displayed a banner with a quote from the communist heroine ("True Freedom is Always the Freedom of the Non-conformists"), they were immediately arrested and exiled from the country.[75]

Finally, tensions between East Germany and her resentful neighbors had reached a breaking

---

[72] Timothy Garten Ash. "The Fall of the Berlin Wall: What it Meant to Be There." The Guardian. 6 November 2014. Web.
[73] Large 520.
[74] Ibid.
[75] Large, 520.

point. With literally tens of thousands of East German refugees clogging the streets, highways, and embassies of her neighbor nations, it was up to East Germany to ease travel restrictions and make some concessions to stem the tide, so the decision was made to allow travel outside of East Berlin for one month to those with proper passports. Large notes that the number of East Germans with proper passports was so low that this would not have caused a high influx of travel outside of the borders. However, the hastily called press conference and the rewriting of the policy up to the last hour meant that a mistake would be made that would change the world as the Germans knew it.

Guenter Schabowski was the official spokesperson at a press conference that was being televised live throughout East Germany. Charged with delivering the new travel guidelines in a hastily-called press conference, Schabowski began his remarks: "You see, comrades, I was informed today…that such an announcement had been…distributed earlier today. You should actually have it already…1) 'Applications for travel abroad by private individuals can now be made without the previously existing requirements (of demonstrating a need to travel or proving familial relationships). The travel authorizations will be issued within a short time. Grounds for denial will only be applied in particular exceptional cases. The responsible departments of passport and registration control in the People's Police district offices in the GDR are instructed to issue visas for permanent exit without delays and without presentation of the existing requirements for permanent exit.'"

After being asked when it would come into effect, Schabowski replied, "That comes into effect, according to my information, immediately, without delay." When asked if it also applies for West Berlin, he responded, "Permanent exit can take place via all border crossings from the GDR to the FRG and West Berlin, respectively."[76]

---

[76] Guenter Schabowski, "Guenter Schabowski's Press Conference in the GDR International Press Center," Making the History of 1989, Item #449, http://chnm.gmu.edu/1989/items/show/449 (accessed February 27 2015, 8:28 pm).

**Picture of the press conference**

*The Wall Street Journal* speculated that Schabowski had faltered not because he had not prepared carefully enough, as some charged, but because he was "not used to scrutiny by a free press...[And] he couldn't deal with rapid-fire questions from international journalists".[77] Whatever the real cause of Schabowski's struggle to communicate, it became immediately clear that "seeming accidents have the power to shape history".[78] Later, American journalist Tom Brokaw would recall following Schakowsky upstairs after the conference had concluded and asking him to re-read the portion of the brief that lifted the travel restrictions on border crossings between East and West Berlin directly. It was then, Brokaw realized, that the end of the Berlin Wall had come. In his newscast, he told the watching world, "This is a historic night.... The East German Government has just declared that East German citizens will be able to cross the wall ... without restrictions."[79] Schabowski would be expelled from the party but fail to escape prosecution as a high Politburo official; he served only a few months of a three-year sentence after distancing himself from communist ideals.

On the evening of November 9th, 1989, Harald Jaeger, an East German border guard, watched

---

[77] Walker, Marcus. "Did Journalists' Questions Topple the Berlin Wall?" The Wall Street Journal. 7 November 2014.

[78] Stern 459.

[79] Melvyn P. Leffler, "Chapter 5: Dreams of Freedom, Temptations of Power," in The Fall of the Berlin Wall: The Revolutionary Legacy of 1989, ed. Jeffrey A. Engel (New York: Oxford University Press, 2009), 136,

a television as he ate a meal at the canteen before arriving for his guard duty shift at the Berlin Wall that night at 6:00 p.m. Hearing the removal of travel restrictions would take place "immediately", he remembers "almost choking on my bread roll". He arrived at the wall to find other skeptical guards and made multiple telephone calls to his superiors, attempting to get clarification about what to do with the now gathering crowds. At first, Jaeger's superiors simply ignored his question, telling them to send people without authorization home. After realizing the seriousness of the situation, however, Jaeger was instructed to let the "most agitated" members of the crowd pass through to West Berlin in hopes of appeasing them. Obviously, the opposite effect was achieved and Jaeger had no further instruction from his superiors. Fearing for the safety of the burgeoning crowd, Jaeger delivered the order to open the border between East and West Berlin at 11:30 p.m.[80] Thus, Jaeger is most often credited with being the man who actually "took down" the Wall.

Another East German border guard, Erich Wittman, recalled his memory of the evening: "I was promoted to Corporal, and was directly posted as the Officer of the main checkpoint of the Berlin wall. I still remember the tensions, thousands of cars was in front of me, honking and wanted me to move, which I refused....The news of the Berlin wall being open for anyone hadn't reached us who were posted at the wall, only when my girlfriend, who I for the first time on [sic] months seen, came to me and told me about it. I was in shock and didn't know what to do, all around me, thousands of people started to gather around me, climbing over the wall, some even brought tools and sledge-hammers and started to destroy the wall, the people kept yelling at us as we told them to stay back, then...On the TV, which I saw through the window of the Guard's Resting place, I could see the politicians ordering the opening to West Berlin for everyone, I ordered the soldiers to open the gates and let the cars pass, the yells formed into cheers and all over us, people came to hug me and my men, and the cars kept swarming over the border. Erika grabbed onto my uniform, and pulled me to her, and hugged me, I responded in kissing her, then a camera man appeared on the scene and filmed the opening of the wall, and got us on tape...The supreme officer came to me later, asked me why the people are flooding over to West Germany, I told him. The German Democratic Republic is dead, they announced it on Television, open your borders as well for these people. He quickly went away, and all over East Germany the news came, and the Berlin wall was flooded by people over several days."

---

[80] "Former border guard Harald Jaeger recalls how he opened the Berlin Wall." South China Morning Post. 6 November 2014.

**A crane removing pieces of the wall in December 1989**

**Pictures of East Germans talking to West Germans through the wall in late November 1989**

**1990 picture of the graffiti and pieces of the wall chipped away**

Even in the wake of the Berlin Wall's end, there was no focal point for revolution in Romania until the unrest in Timișoara. The city, in the east of Romania, was home to a Hungarian minority that had been oppressed within the country, and as with several of the revolutions, the church proved of crucial importance. One priest, László Tőkés, was attracting large congregations due to his veiled criticism of Ceaușescu and the communist regime. The priest had criticised Ceaușescu's forced "Systemisation Policy," moving people from the countryside to cities and towns against their will.[81] In response, the authorities, believing that Tőkés was being subversive, attempted to evict him from his position. This brought protests from the Hungarians, which was met by force from the Securitate.

---

[81] Brendan Simms, *Europe: The Struggle for Supremacy 1453 to the Present* (London: Penguin, 2014), p. 482.

The protestors took to the streets of Timișoara on December 16, 1989, and over the next two days the security forces took part in a brutal crackdown, killing around 100 protestors. Rumors spread around the country that the death toll was in the thousands, and in the mistaken belief that the situation was under control, Ceaușescu left the country on December 18 for a visit to Iran. It was Elena Ceaușescu and the security services who were given the responsibility to quell the Timișoara disturbances.

As the unrest grew more violent, Ceaușescu returned to Bucharest on December 20 faced with a growing crisis. The dictator, however, had lost touch with his country long before and had no idea that the situation was as dangerous as it proved. Oblivious to the anger that had welled up against him, a crushing taste of reality came on December 21. The Romanian leader called a rally of 100,000 people to Palace Square, many of whom had been coerced to attend by party apparatchiks, and Ceaușescu then addressed the crowd with a typically stuttering and turgid speech, condemning the Timișoara protestors and reeling off the usual communist tropes. When parts of the crowd began chanting "Timișoara," Ceaușescu offered to increase pensions by a paltry amount. This further enraged the crowd, who then turned on Ceaușescu, attempting to storm the building and quickly descending into chaos. Videocameras captured the events and aptly show Ceaușescu's reaction. He looked completely bemused and lost for a response.

On that fateful day, the usually compliant crowd had been so moved as to chant "Down with the Murderers!"[82] As the mood became feverish, the regime suddenly began to shake. What kept Ceaușescus in place was the support of a stupefied party and the armed forces, but all of it dissolved within the space of a few hours. The day after the Palace Square speech, with protests spreading, the army crucially joined in with the demonstrators, in effect switching sides and abandoning Ceaușescu.

With the revolution fully underway, Ceaușescu and his wife fled Bucharest by helicopter, but as it became apparent that every element of the Romanian establishment supported his removal, even the helicopter pilot abandoned the couple. Thus, they were marooned in rural Romania with one bodyguard who remained loyal to the end. The trio held a car up at gunpoint, commandeering it and forcing the driver to speed away to possible safety.

Meanwhile, revolutionaries and military men took charge of the state broadcasters, informing the country of the couple's flight and urging their capture. The driver told the pair that they could take refuge in a factory building, but once they were there, he called for help and the police came to take them into custody.

The end for Nicolae and Elena Ceaușescu was remarkably swift. The new power brokers, led by the "National Salvation Front" in Bucharest, organised a hasty show trial, during which

[82] Godfrey Hodgson, *People's Century: From the dawn of the century to the eve of the millennium* (Godalming: BBC Books, 1998), p. 596.

Nicolae and Elena were tried and convicted of a range of crimes and sentenced the death. They were executed by firing squad on Christmas Day. Ironically, capital punishment was abolished the following year by the post-communist government.

The manner in which Ceaușescu and his wife were executed was widely criticized by foreign observers, and the footage of the trials, executions, and corpses shocked many. Everyone was aware of the cruel nature of the Ceaușescu regime, but the new leaders of Romania made little effort to rise above the merciless ways that preceded them.

Needless to say, Romania was terribly impoverished by the end of Ceaușescu's time in power, and compared to its contemporaries, Romania has found it awfully difficult to overcome its communist legacy.

One of the regime's most obvious legacies consisted of Romanian orphanages, and to make matters worse, Romania had used inadequate, often unsterile medical supplies during the 1980s. As a result, AIDS became prevalent in the country, so much so that by the time Nicolae was deposed, half the children in Europe who had AIDs were Romanian.[83] During the 1990s, Romania remained closely associated with the orphan issue, and the country's people were a subject of pity. To date, Romania and Moldova have been widely considered by many as the poorest and least developed of the former communist states in Central Europe and Eastern Europe, and both Romanians and Moldovans have migrated en masse since the end of the Cold War. Although Romanians did not have free movement within the European Union (EU) until 2013, many now live in other countries, most notably Italy. The root cause for this has been the miserable condition of the Romanian economy, which Ceaușescu hollowed out, particularly during his final decade in office, with merciless austerity. It has proven very difficult for governments in Romania to overcome this handicap despite significant assistance from the EU.

The governing coalition that emerged after Ceaușescu's death, the National Salvation Front (NSF), was led by former communist official Ion Iliescu, and the NSF initiated many of the same reforms as other former communist regimes undergoing the transition to a market-based democracy in the 1990s. Romania held elections in May 1990, with Iliescu and the NSF taking power and a new constitution being drafted and signed the following year. With that, Romania moved tentatively towards democratic institutions, rule of law, more liberal values and a market economy.

However, all of these pillars have been met with challenges. Corruption has been a constant issue in Romanian politics, and the economy, although making progress, has consistently failed to generate enough wealth to significantly lift standards of living across the country. There are plenty of reasons for this, and many go back to the Ceaușescu era. Most notably, there was no

---

[83] Godfrey Hodgson, *People's Century: From the dawn of the century to the eve of the millennium* (Godalming: BBC Books, 1998), p. 597.

opposition movement to speak of before 1989, unlike countries such as Poland and Czechoslovakia. Ceaușescu's Securitate was so intrusive that it proved impossible for dissent to coalesce around individuals or groups.[84] Furthermore, although many Romanians hated the president and his wife, there was little active backing for a Western-style government, which meant the reforms of the 1990s had little public support.[85] Observers of Romanian politics believe that the 1990s reforms did not go far enough to present a significant break with the past, and as a result, the country has stagnated for much of the post-Ceaușescu period. The dictator himself may have been quickly disposed of, but his sepcter still haunted the country for years. A lack of transparency, real economic reform and endemic corruption are just a few examples.

For many, the execution of Ceaușescu offered great hope, but ultimately it became considered as a "false dawn."[86] Romania's post-Ceaușescu leaders have, for the most part, been former communists, and critics have even complained that the revolution was little more than a "palace coup."[87] As was common in the region after 1989, liberal economic measures were enacted, such as deregulation and privatization, but the latter policy made a handful of opportunists very rich as they capitalized on ownership rights over former state-controlled enterprises and industries.

Romania has certainly made advancements in the wake of Ceaușescu's death. In 2004, the country became a member of NATO, and in 2007 it became a member of the EU. Romania joined the continent's Human Rights institution, the Council of Europe, as early as 1993. However, the country has struggled economically despite an increase in its average wealth; for example, its GDP per capita is now approximately half that of the Czech Republic, another former communist country. Romania now styles itself as a base for low cost manufacturing, services, and a vibrant technology sector, but many of the problems associated with the Ceaușescu era – not least corruption – persist, to the detriment of the country.

Such is the frustration that many Romanians have with the post-Cold War era that many now have more positive opinions of the former dictator. In 2014, an opinion poll of Romanians indicated that 60% of surveyed respondents thought life was better under communism.[88] This is similar to trends found across Central Europe and Eastern Europe. This phenomenon was dubbed *Ostalgie* by Germans, or nostalgia for the east.

---

[84] Vladimir Tismaneanu, 'Romania's First Post-Communist Decade: From Iliescu to Iliescu', Wilson Center, 7 July 2011, https://www.wilsoncenter.org/publication/225-romanias-first-post-communist-decade-iliescu-to-iliescu, [accessed 19 November 2018]

[85] Ibid.

[86] Emma Graham-Harrison, "Twenty-five years after Nicolae Ceaușescu was executed, Romanians seek a 'revolution reborn'", *The Guardian*, 7 December 2014, https://www.theguardian.com/world/2014/dec/07/romanians-seek-a-reborn-revolution-25-years-after-Ceaușescu, [accessed 19 November 2018]

[87] Ibid.

[88] Vlad Odobescu, 'Nicolae Ceaușescu's legacy reconsidered amid nostalgia for communism in Romania', *The Washington Post* 18 April 2016, https://www.washingtontimes.com/news/2016/apr/18/nicolae-Ceaușescus-legacy-reconsidered-amid-nostal/, [accessed 19 November 2018]

It is true that the early years of Ceaușescu's rule did see some real benefits for Romanians. The economy grew, society was a bit freer than before, and the country's place in the world became more prestigious. Ceaușescu stood up to the Soviets after the 1968 invasion of Czechoslovakia, and his nationalist policies proved popular. On the other hand, it is hard to imagine that Ceaușescu's regime could generate much objective praise, and historians continue to justifiably consider him one of the region's most incompetent and callous dictators.

If anything, it is easy to forget that Romania had a number of things going for it when Nicolae Ceaușescu took power in 1965. The Romanians could boast of resources, raw materials and an important strategic location that had allowed leaders to carve out an "independent" foreign policy. Furthermore, Ceaușescu initially seemed to mark a step forward in the country's socialist development, and he had the kind of background that could have compelled a better man to be an effective leader for his people. His early life had been marked by poverty and struggle, during which he found meaning in communist ideology, and he believed strongly enough in the ideology that he engaged in underground activities in the 1930s and survived imprisonment for them. He had also shown promise as an efficient bureaucrat under Gheorghe Gheorghiu-Dej.

In the end, however, he left Romania in such an awful condition that while it took less than a week for him to lose his absolute grip on power in December 1989, it will end up taking more than 30 years for his country to rebound.


## Yugoslavia's Dissolution

Yugoslavia had straddled the line between economic frailty and independent prosperity throughout its history. Tito had managed to secure loans and financial aid from the West while retaining close relations - and therefore trade - with the communist bloc. Indeed, Yugoslavia was a rare example of a country that traded with both east and west. As a result, GDP per capita was higher in Yugoslavia than many of its contemporaries in Central Europe and Eastern Europe.

The Yugoslav model was seen by many as an acceptable socialist system, particularly considering its arrangement of local worker control over factories and production, but by the end of the 1980s, it was suffering from similar problems facing other communist countries. This was due to a combination of the world recession in the early 1980s and resulting high interest rates (and related hikes in interest payments and debt), as well as chronically low productivity, high unemployment, and emigration to other European countries.[89] In the late 1980s Yugoslavia went into a severe recession, made worse by mounting levels of debt. The IMF was called in to provide an emergency loan, and Yugoslavia had already received debt relief in 1983 and 1984, a particularly acute point in its crisis after a campaign by the American-led group "Friends of

---

[89] Ann Lane, *Yugoslavia: When Ideals Collide*, (Basingstoke: Palgrave Macmillan, 2004), p. 158.

Yugoslavia."[90]

The Cold War came to a sudden climax in 1989 when the Berlin Wall fell, and the special geopolitical position of Yugoslavia was now redundant. American political scientist Francis Fukuyama famously declared that this marked the "End of History,"[91] and that the world was now moving into a period of universal liberal democracy and market capitalism. "Washington Consensus" was coined to describe the pro-market policies pursued by the likes of the IMF and World Bank. When the Soviet Union dissolved formally in 1991, the West had seemingly triumphed in its confrontation against communism, and there would be no room for even hybrid models such as Yugoslavia's. Indeed, Yugoslavia was quickly put into this new paradigm, at least in the economic sphere. As with so many other examples during the period, a sclerotic, low growth and low productivity economy was prescribed a tough dose of austerity and liberalization in return for emergency financial assistance.

The role this "structural adjustment" program played in the onset of violence in Yugoslavia has been disputed. Some believe that it simply increased unhappiness about the status quo and heralded a more rapid disintegration of the Federation. Others believed that the IMF package was the last opportunity Yugoslavia had to reform.

The man in charge of its implementation was Ante Marković. Marković was a Bosnian Croat who had fought with Tito's Partisans during the Second World War. A communist, Marković had been President of Croatia from 1986-1988, and he became Yugoslav Prime Minister in March 1989. It is perhaps ironic then that Marković would be entrusted with implementing this most capitalist set of policies.

Despite his background, Marković was an enthusiastic economic reformer, believing the IMF package was necessary.[92] Marković tied the currency (the Dinar) to the German Mark, attempting state privatization and trade liberalization.[93] Although the initial results were uneven, Marković's reforms did appear to curb inflation and improve incomes. He was also popular and one of the last prominent pan-Yugoslav politicians of any heft. Marković was sharply critical of the leaders who had swerved towards nationalism, including Milošević, as well as Borisav Jović in Serbia and Radovan Karadžić in Bosnia and Herzegovina. Marković was both a man of the future and the past, committed not only to economic reform and a better standard of living for Yugoslavs but also rooted in the socialist view of the country as a fraternal enterprise. He was, however, unsuited to the atmosphere of Yugoslavia in its final phase, a time in which most nominally communist politicians had retreated behind nationalist shields. He desperately tried to

---

[90] John R. Lampe, *Yugoslavia as History. Twice there was a country*. (Cambridge: Cambridge University Press, 2000), pp. 322-323.

[91] Francis Fukuyama, 'The End of History?', *The National Interest*, No. 16 (Summer 1989), pp. 3-18.

[92] John R. Lampe, *Yugoslavia as History. Twice there was a country*. (Cambridge: Cambridge University Press, 2000), pp. 352-355.

[93] Carole Rogel, *The Breakup of Yugoslavia and its Aftermath* (London: Greenwood Press, 2004), p. 21.

curtail the descent into conflict in 1990 and 1991, but the politicians around him had already drawn the battle lines.

**Marković**

The most visible moment before conflicts engulfed Yugoslavia was the 1990 Communist Party Congress, officially termed the 14th Congress of the League of Communists of Yugoslavia, which took place in Belgrade in late January 1990. The congress was called as an extraordinary meeting to discuss the various political disputes that had arisen since the previous meeting in 1986. With the Cold War quickly winding down, the different parties reverted to previous inclinations at the congress. The main dispute was between the Serbian and Slovenian delegations over the former's centralization proposals, whereas the latter wanted more autonomy for the republics. The Serbs made a number of proposals for which they could now achieve majority decisions. Milošević's manoeuvring since 1987 meant that he had, essentially, appointees and allies in charge of the Kosovo, Vojvodina, and Montenegro delegations, as well as his own Serb party. This meant Milošević commanded a bloc vote that could pass or strike down any decision he chose.

The congress dragged on for two days, full of arguments, rows, and disagreements. Milan Kučan told the Serb delegation that he needed at least the appearance of compromise over his suggestions. When this proved not to be forthcoming, the Slovenian delegation resigned and stormed out of the convention hall. Initially, the Croats were unsure of what to do and Milošević tried to persuade them to remain, knowing he could still maintain the semblance of unity even without the Slovenes. Nevertheless, after some deliberation, the Croats joined the Slovenes by leaving. The delegations from Macedonia and Bosnia and Herzegovina followed.

Whether this was all by Milošević's design or an unintended effect of his aggressive actions is hard to discern, but either way, the League was now dead.[94] The country itself was now in serious peril, decoupled as it was from the socialist ideology that had bound it together for 45 years. Socialist ideology was giving way to the nationalist variety, and this movement clearly pointed to self-determination and democracy in other communist countries. The end of the Cold War and the winds of change that swept through the continent would prove more problematic in Yugoslavia, a country with so many sectarian identities.

Yugoslavia limped on throughout 1990. Without the League, the Federation was exposed even more to nationalist unrest. It was not possible for every republic to simply split from the Federation, however. Slovenia may have been mostly Slovene, but there was a significant minority of Serbs in Croatia and Kosovo. Ethnic Albanians made up a sizeable minority in Macedonia, while Bosnia and Herzegovina were almost equally divided three ways between the majority Bosnian Muslims (or Bosniaks), Bosnian Serbs, and Bosnian Croats. Independence into nationalist states unnerved the minorities, which then looked towards their majority republic for protection. This then led to ideas of Greater Croatia and Greater Serbia, which implied some territorial conquest. The number of people who identified as "Yugoslav," as opposed to their individual nationalities, was in steep decline, and only significant in number in the most ethnically-mixed republic, Bosnia and Herzegovina.[95]

Despite the issues, some political reforms took place in the country's final days. Elections were held on April 8, 1990 in each republic, the first since the 1940s. Nationalists and independence-minded parties swept the elections. Franjo Tudjman's hard-line Croatian Democratic Union (HDZ) party won in Croatia by promising to "defend" the republic from Milošević. This led to Belgrade endorsing resistance to the HDZ, or as Belgrade put it, the NDH. Croatian Serbs in Knin, in the Krajina area, led by police inspector Milan Martić, formed a militia and seized control of the region. A sizeable section of Croatia was now effectively outside the control of Tudjman's government in Zagreb. The Serb-dominated Yugoslav National Army (JNA), meanwhile, was guaranteeing the security of Serb minorities outside Serbia.

In late 1990 and early 1991 conflict had essentially begun in Krajina and was looming elsewhere in the Federation. Ante Marković was desperately trying to stabilise Yugoslavia's economy, even as his country would soon start losing its component parts.

The first to leave was Slovenia, which was never considered the most problematic of Yugoslavia's republics. One of the three key founder members in 1918 as part of the Kingdom of Serbs, Croats and Slovenes, the crucial confrontations had consistently been between Serbia and Croatia, whereas Slovenes saw themselves as more "European" than the other more "Balkan" republics. Slovenia had been part of the Austro-Hungarian Empire and therefore more a part of "civilized" Central Europe. It was also the only Catholic region in Yugoslavia besides Croatia. Slovenia's language was also different than the other republics, where Serbo-Croat dominated.

[94] Carole Rogel, *The Breakup of Yugoslavia and its Aftermath* (London: Greenwood Press, 2004), pp. 18-19.
[95] Vesna Drapac, *Constructing Yugoslavia: A Transnational History*, (Basingstoke: Palgrave Macmillan, 2010), p. 248.

Many young people in 1980s Slovenia had been behind the push towards greater democratic accountability, and Slovene President Milan Kučan had exploited the tension in Kosovo to promote greater autonomy set apart from central (Serb) domination.

After leading the walkout of the January 1990 congress, it seemed only a matter of time before Slovenia withdrew further support from Belgrade.[96] As the rest of Europe attempted to cope with the challenges presented by the fall of the Berlin Wall, Slovenia prepared to hold a referendum on continuing membership in the Yugoslav Federation. On December 23, Slovenia held its referendum, during which 88% of voters opted for independence.

Distracted by events elsewhere in Yugoslavia, Belgrade was slow to respond. Although this did not energize nationalists in the same way it would've if Bosnia and Herzegovina or Kosovo had declared an intention to break away, the Slovene decision was actually the death knell for Yugoslavia. If it was allowed to leave unimpeded, it would surely only be a matter of time before Croatia declared independence. It was a precedent that contained its own logic.

Six months later, on June 25, 1991, Slovenia declared formal independence, and in response, the Yugoslav authorities dispatched the JNA to prevent the Slovene breakaway. Slovenia had few troops or military equipment, save the Slovene sections of the federal army, called the Slovenian Territorial Defence (TO). In a straight fight between the JNA and the Slovene forces, it would have been no contest.

A number of issues ensured that the so-called "Ten Day War" was by far the least destructive of the conflicts that gripped Yugoslavia throughout the 1990s. Most importantly, the JNA relied on the Serbs, who had to travel through Croatia and who were by no means supportive of the action. The soldiers had little incentive to fight, with the ethnicity issue neutralized in the case of Slovenia. Furthermore, there was no official force as such to fight; the TO had been organized into guerrilla fighting units, ready to engage in asymmetric warfare with 21,000 personnel.

On June 26, 1991 the Yugoslav army moved into Slovenia and came into contact with TO militias.[97] Slovene politicians immediately attempted to garner international support for their independence, and against the Yugoslav army's actions. The United Nations called for an end to the fighting, with this pressure bearing almost immediate fruit. The Yugoslavs were persuaded to come to the negotiating table, and a ceasefire was announced on July 2. Five days later, an agreement was signed on the island of Brioni, incidentally one of Tito's favorite residences, to bring the fighting to an official end. The "Brioni Accord" recognized Slovene independence and ended the short war. During the fighting, 44 Yugoslav soldiers and 18 Slovene TO troops had been killed. These casualty figures would be dwarfed by the later Balkan wars, a sign that other

---

[96] Carole Rogel, *The Breakup of Yugoslavia and its Aftermath* (London: Greenwood Press, 2004), pp. 18-19.
[97] John Tagliabue, 'Yugoslav Army Uses Force in Breakaway Republic; Slovenia Reports 100 Wounded or Killed', *The New York Times*, 28 June 1991, https://www.nytimes.com/1991/06/28/world/yugoslav-army-uses-force-breakaway-republic-slovenia-reports-100-wounded-killed.html, [accessed 31 October 1991]

nationalist leaders may have thought that leaving Yugoslavia would be relatively straightforward after Slovenia.

Slovene independence was not immediately recognized by the international community, which was unsure of how to respond to nationalist agitation in Yugoslavia. It would be another six months, in January 1992 when Slovene independence was widely recognized and almost a year until it was accepted as a member of the United Nations. By this point, conflict was raging across the Federation, firstly in Croatia and then in Bosnia and Herzegovina.

The Croats had generally sided with the Slovenes as internecine politics emerged in the late 1980s. With Ljubljana exiting Yugoslavia in 1990-1991, it was clear that many Croat nationalists would also want independence. Franjo Tudjman had positioned himself as the leader of the separatists by this time, and his HDZ party had already won an electoral victory in 1990.

Croatia, however, was a far more complex issue. The main point of tension throughout Yugoslavia's history had in fact been between Serbs and Croats. This had manifested itself in the 1920s, when a Serb had assassinated the popular Croat politician Stjepan Radić. The Ustaše leader Ante Pavelić successfully plotted to murder Yugoslav King Alexander in 1934, and during the Second World War, the Nazi-backed Croat state, the NDH regime, had terrorized other Yugoslav nationalities, most significantly the Serbs. The animosity had remerged during the Croatian Spring unrest in the 1960s and 1970s. As central authority broke down in the Yugoslav Federation in the late 1980s, therefore, it did not take long for suspicion to increase between Serbs and Croats.

Separation would be difficult for Tudjman and his allies. First, Croatia contained a large Serb minority, and some Serbs had already taken matters into their own hands during the uprising in Knin in Krajina in 1990. Belgrade feared, correctly, that Croat troops would attempt to retake the enclave by force, while the Croats worried that Milošević was developing a Greater Serbia project. The Serbian strongman had by now fashioned a reputation as a defender of the Serbs, and he seemed unlikely to allow such a large number of Serbs to break away into a separate state that was potentially hostile to their interests.[98] Unlike in Slovenia, any political move would likely trigger a military response from the JNA, which by now was the only arbiter of order within the Federation. This was problematic since it was increasingly seen as a Serb-dominated army.[99]

Tension rose in early 1991 when the "Špegelj Tapes" were uncovered by Yugoslav media. They appeared to record the Croatian Defence Minister, Martin Špegelj, arranging the shipment of arms to Croat depots via Hungary. The revelation heightened fears that Croatia was about to

[98] Tom Buchanan, *Europe's Troubled Peace. 1945 to the Present* (Chichester: Wiley-Blackwell, 2012, 2nd ed), p. 242.

[99] John R. Lampe, *Yugoslavia as History. Twice there was a country* (Cambridge: Cambridge University Press, 2000), p. 332.

break away from the rest of the Federation. An independence referendum was then held on May 2, 1991, with 93% of voters opting for autonomy. Tudjman subsequently declared independence on June 25, the same day as the Slovenes.

While Slovenia successfully left after a short war, Croatia would face a much tougher departure. In fact, Croatia would be at war for over four years. Milošević's argument to the Croats was that the principle of self-determination should apply to Serbs in the country, therefore giving them the option to separate from the rest of Croatia. This was obviously anathema to the Croat leadership.

There were some large regions of majority-Serb populations. One was the Krajina, which included Knin and bordered Serb-dominated parts of Bosnia and Herzegovina. The others were Western Slavonia and Eastern Slavonia, in the northeast of Croatia and bordering Serbia. All three areas were backed by Serbia, supplied with weapons and diplomatic support. They soon declared themselves autonomous regions, outside the sovereignty of any Croat state.

Fighting had broken out between Serbs and Croats in Plitvice in April 1991, an area of conjoining lakes popular among tourists, but this low-level conflict expanded into a full-scale war. Nominally protecting Serbs in the autonomous regions, the JNA moved on the major coastal Croatian cities of Split and Dubrovnik in the summer of 1991 after the independence declaration.[100] By shelling these cities indiscriminately, the JNA was besieging the Croats and terrorizing their populations, attempting to extort political concessions from Zagreb. At the time, the JNA claimed it was targeting Ustaše terrorists in both cities.

Following this initial reasoning, the Serbs and their allies the Montenegrins set their sights on capturing the ancient city of Dubrovnik. Both Split and Dubrovnik were hugely popular with Western tourists. The latter was dubbed the "Pearl of the Adriatic," and therefore a significant source of foreign currency for Croatia. The sieges hit the fledgling Croatian state financially and in terms of prestige, and the fighting caused cultural vandalism in the process. This latter point was probably important in the swift international condemnation that was aimed at Belgrade and the Yugoslav leadership from the international community.

Shortly after Slovenia and Croatia declared independence in June 1991 and fighting erupted, the United Nations and European Community sought to intervene diplomatically. The Europeans, shocked by the first major violence on the continent in years, scrambled to respond. Aware that the United States wanted to quell the violence, the Europeans took center stage instead. Confident after the fall of the Berlin Wall, and with the Community about to expand into the European Union, one foreign minister, Jacques Poos, hubristically proclaimed the "Hour of Europe" had come. As a result, the European Community deployed negotiators, former British

---

[100] Chuck Sudetic, 'Shelling of Besieged Yugoslav Port Is Intensified', *The New York Times*, 13 November 1991, https://www.nytimes.com/1991/11/13/world/shelling-of-besieged-yugoslav-port-is-intensified.html, [accessed 31 October 2018]

Foreign Secretary Lord Carrington and Portuguese diplomat José Cutileiro, to reach a diplomatic solution.[101]

The conflict in Croatia soon developed an internal Hobbesian logic. Although a federal Yugoslavia still nominally existed, when Slovenia and Croatia declared independence, Belgrade, the JNA, and the Federation basically came to resemble nothing more than a rump state of Serbia. As the JNA moved in to prevent Slovenia and Croatia from leaving the Federation, and also to protect Serbs in Krajina and Slavonia, the mandate appeared to shift. The longer the fighting dragged on, the more it looked as if the JNA was an agent for Serb domination and even conquest.

As Dubrovnik remained under siege, the JNA turned its attention to the Croatian city of Vukovar. With a mixed population of Serbs and Croats, Vukovar lay to the east of Croatia, within the Serb-declared region of Eastern Slavonia. After the declaration of Serb Krajina earlier in 1991, Vukovar became a focal point for tension between Serbs and Croats in the region. Barricades were erected, militias formed, and fighting broke out between groups soon afterwards. The Croat authorities sent forces of under 2,000 to defend the city from a JNA or Serb militia takeover. After the declaration of independence by Zagreb, fighting in and around Vukovar worsened and the JNA did indeed surround the city. From early October 1991, the JNA besieged Vukovar, pummelling it with shells and attempting to starve its inhabitants into submission. The Croat forces defending the city launched offensives against the JNA but were hopelessly outnumbered. JNA troops numbered 36,000, an overwhelming advantage.

The JNA launched their own offensive in November 1991 and took control of the city from the Croats. What followed was chilling, and a harbinger for later events in Bosnia and Herzegovina. In their acclaimed book, *The Death of Yugoslavia*, authors Laura Silber and Allan Little described the aftermath of the Battle of Vukovar as a horrific scene of corpses, chaos and destruction.[102] The Croat population of around 20,000 was forced to leave the city, their homes were looted, and a number of massacres and rapes were carried out by the attacking forces. Many Croats were taken prisoner and detained. Vukovar and its aftermath set the pattern for much of the subsequent fighting, and the city itself would be part of the self-proclaimed Serb Krajina republic until 1995, when Croats retook control of Vukovar.

The negotiators finally brought pressure to bear on the Yugoslavs and the JNA at the end of 1991. A ceasefire was declared in January 1992, and the UN deployed peacekeepers as part of its UN Protection Force (UNPROFOR). The UN "Blue Helmets" were mandated to protect the population in three areas, called "Safe Havens." As a result, the conflict in Croatia was frozen

---

[101] Alan Riding, 'Conflict in Yugoslavia; Europeans send high-level team', *The New York Times*, 29 June 1991, https://www.nytimes.com/1991/06/29/world/conflict-in-yugoslavia-europeans-send-high-level-team.html, [accessed 31 October 2018]

[102] Laura Silber and Allan Little, *The Death of Yugoslavia* (London: Penguin, 1996), p. 180.

until the summer of 1995.

The UN and its Security Council had been dormant for much of the Cold War, but now that the superpower confrontation was over, more decisions could be passed without a veto. The early 1990s were a period when the West, now led by a sole superpower, could attempt to mold the international landscape in its image. The UN wanted to enforce international law, self-determination, and human rights standards in Yugoslavia, but there was no consensus on the best approach in the Balkans after 1991. Events in the region threw up devilishly complex challenges where liberal principles contradicted each other. After all, how could national self-determination be applied in ethnically and nationally mixed societies? What was an appropriate use of external force to restore order and prevent further violence? How could minority rights be secured in the successor states? These issues would be hotly debated over the course of the 1990s and only reach some kind of consensus by the time of the Kosovo crisis in 1998-1999.

Yugoslavia only formally folded in 2006 after Montenegrins voted in a referendum to leave the Federation, though in reality, Yugoslavia had not truly existed for several years. Today, the states of the former Yugoslavia are either EU members or candidates. The latter face huge challenges to fulfill this ambition. Apart from the often authoritarian and corrupt political systems in place, these states need to resolve outstanding territorial claims before they can achieve membership. Needless to say, the hangover caused by the disintegration of Yugoslavia has turned out to be long and painful.

The demise of Yugoslavia disconcerted Western society and led to much soul-searching after the fact. Many wondered how a country that seemed financially successful for long stretches could come apart at the seams so quickly and spectacularly. But as any examination of the complete history of the state demonstrates, it faced significant challenges from its very inception. Perhaps the story of Yugoslavia should focus more on how the multinational state survived as long as it did.

**Online Resources**

Other books about 20<sup>th</sup> century history by Charles River Editors

Other books about Tito on Amazon

Other books about Ceausescu on Amazon

### Further Reading about Tito

Banac, Ivo. *With Stalin Against Tito: Cominformist Splits in Yugoslav Communism*. Ithaca, 1988.

Dedijer, Vladimir. *Tito*. New York, 1953.

Greentree, David. *Knight's Move: the Hunt for Marshal Tito 1944.* Botley, 2012.

Kerner, Robert J. (editor). *Yugoslavia.* Berkeley, 1949.

Kurowski, Franz. *The Brandenburger Commandos: Germany's Elite Warrior Spies in World War II.* Mechanicsburg, 2005.

Lees, Lorraine M. *Keeping Tito Afloat: The United States, Yugoslavia, and the Cold War.* University Park, 1997.

Lincoln, Bruce W. *Red Victory: A History of the Russian Civil War, 1918-1921.* New York, 1999.

MacLean, Fitzroy. *The Heretic: The Life and Times of Josip Broz-Tito.* New York, 1957.

Ramet, Sabrina Petra. *Balkan Babel: The Disintegration of Yugoslavia from the Death of Tito to Ethnic War.* Boulder, 1996.

Roberts, Walter E. *Tito, Mihailovic, and the Allies, 1941-1945.* Durham, 1987.

Rogovin, Vadim Z. *Stalin's Terror of 1937-1938: Political Genocide in the USSR.* Oak Park, 2009.

Swain, Geoffrey. *Tito: A Biography.* New York, 2011.

Vuksic, Velimir. *Tito's Partisans 1941-45.* Botley, 2003.

West, Richard. *Tito and the Rise and Fall of Yugoslavia.* New York, 1994.

**Further Reading about Ceausescu**

David A. Andelman, 'Ceausescu, Tito Tread Wary and Parallel Paths', 16 April 1978, *New York Times* https://www.nytimes.com/1978/04/16/archives/ceausescu-tito-tread-wary-and-parallel-paths.html

Ronald D. Bachman (ed.), Romania: A Country Study. "The Ceausescu Era" (Washington: Library of Congress, 1989)

Cornel Ban, 'What brought Romania into Default in 1981?' *European Economics,* 19 May 2012, https://europeaneconomics.wordpress.com/2012/05/19/what-brought-romania-into-default-in-1981/

Raluca Besliu, 'Communist Nostalgia in Romania', *Open Democracy*, 13 April 2014, https://www.opendemocracy.net/can-europe-make-it/raluca-besliu/communist-nostalgia-in-romania

David Binder, 'The Cult of Ceausescu', *New York Times*, 30 November 1986, https://www.nytimes.com/1986/11/30/magazine/the-cult-of-ceausescu.html

Ralph Blumenthal, 'Upheaval in the East: Obituary - The Ceausescus: 24 Years of Fierce Repression, Isolation and Independence', *New York Times*, 26 December 1989, https://www.nytimes.com/1989/12/26/obituaries/upheaval-east-obituary-ceausescus-24-years-fierce-repression-isolation.html

Celestine Bohlen, 'Gorbachev challenged by Romania', *The Washington Post*, 28 May 1987, https://www.washingtonpost.com/archive/politics/1987/05/28/gorbachev-challenged-by-romania/39020705-b8eb-470c-9244-e98f4257ce97/?utm_term=.823b4c8dafb3

R.J. Crampton, *The Balkans since the Second World War*, (Routledge, 2014)

William E. Crowther, *The political economy of Romanian socialism* (Praeger, 1988)

Misha Glenny, *The Balkans 1804-2012: Nationalism, War and the Great Powers* (London: Granta, 2012)

Emma Graham-Harrison, "Twenty-five years after Nicolae Ceausescu was executed, Romanians seek a 'revolution reborn'", *The Guardian*, 7 December 2014, https://www.theguardian.com/world/2014/dec/07/romanians-seek-a-reborn-revolution-25-years-after-ceausescu

Jussi M. Hanhimaki, *The Rise and Fall of Détente. American Foreign Policy and the Transformation of the Cold War,* (Washington DC: Potomac Books, 2012)

Godfrey Hodgson, *People's Century: From the dawn of the century to the eve of the millennium* (Godalming: BBC Books, 1998)

Geoffrey Howe, *Conflict of Loyalty* (Basingstoke: Macmillan, 1994)

Geraint Hughes, *Harold Wilson's Cold War. The Labour Government and East-West Politics, 1964-1970*, (Woodbridge: Boydell and Boydell, 2009)

International Commission on the Holocaust in Romania, "Executive Summary: Historical Findings and Recommendations". *Final Report of the International Commission on the Holocaust in Romania*. Yad Vashem (The Holocaust Martyrs' and Heroes' Remembrance Authority), 11 November 2004.

Sielke Kelner, 'Ceausescu and the Six-Day War: The View from Washington and London', *The Wilson Center*, 5 June 2017, https://www.wilsoncenter.org/blog-post/ceausescu-and-the-six-day-war-the-view-washington-and-london

Michael Ledeen, 'Review of Red Horizons Red Horizons, by Ion Mihai Pacepa', *The American Spectator* April 1988

Sharon Maxwell Magnus, 'Ceauşescu's orphans: what a regressive abortion law does to a country', *The Conversation*, 1 February 2017, https://theconversation.com/ceau-escus-orphans-what-a-regressive-abortion-law-does-to-a-country-71949

Mark Mazower, *The Balkans: From the End of Byzantium to the Present Day* (London: Phoenix, 2001)

'Gorbachev Faults Stalin on Rift With Tito', *The New York Times* 17 March 1988, https://www.nytimes.com/1988/03/17/world/gorbachev-faults-stalin-on-rift-with-tito.html

Vlad Odobescu, 'Nicolae Ceausescu's legacy reconsidered amid nostalgia for communism in Romania', *The Washington Post* 18 April 2016, https://www.washingtontimes.com/news/2016/apr/18/nicolae-ceausescus-legacy-reconsidered-amid-nostal/

Ion Mihai Pacepa *Red Horizons: The True Story of Nicolae and Elena Ceauşescu's' Crimes, Lifestyle, and Corruption,* (Regnery, 1990)

Mark Percival, 'Britain's "Political Romance" with Romania in the 1970s', *Contemporary European History* (4, no. 1 (1995) pp. 67-87)

Brendan Simms, *Europe: The Struggle for Supremacy 1453 to the Present* (London: Penguin, 2014)

John Simpson, 'Ten Days that Fooled the World', *The Independent* 16 December 1994, https://www.independent.co.uk/life-style/ten-days-that-fooled-the-world-1387659.html

Cezar Stanciu, 'A Rebirth of Diplomacy: The Foreign Policy of Communist Romania between Subordination and Autonomy, 1948–1962', *Diplomacy & Statecraft*, (24:2, 2013, pp. 253-272)

Wendell Steavenson, 'Ceausescu's children', *The Guardian*, 10 December 2014, https://www.theguardian.com/news/2014/dec/10/-sp-ceausescus-children

James R. Stocker, 'A Historical Inevitability?: Kissinger and US Contacts with the Palestinians (1973–76)', *The International History Review*, (39:2, 2017, pp. 316-337)

Vladimir Tismaneanu, 'Romania's First Post-Communist Decade: From Iliescu to Iliescu', Wilson Center, 7 July 2011, https://www.wilsoncenter.org/publication/225-romanias-first-post-communist-decade-iliescu-to-iliescu

## Free Books by Charles River Editors

We have brand new titles available for free most days of the week. To see which of our titles are currently free, click on this link.

## Discounted Books by Charles River Editors

We have titles at a discount price of just 99 cents everyday. To see which of our titles are currently 99 cents, click on this link.

Made in United States
Orlando, FL
09 October 2022

23172577R00070